Social Security:

The New Rules, Essentials & Maximizing Your Social Security, Retirement, Medicare, Pensions & Benefits Explained In One Place

Book Description

Today, most people are talking about Social Security, but they do not know the importance of enrolling in this program. It is important for you to understand how the Social Security program works if you are really serious about your retirement plan. Do not live a miserable life. After seeing how people suffer in their lives, even after working for several years, I decided to come up with this book to enable you to realize why people need to enroll in the Social Security program.

Social Security benefits and Medicare play a significant part in your future financial well-being. Therefore, instead of assuming about this program, it will be rather important for you to read this book and understand this program, what it offers to recipients, how you can benefit from it, and what it does not offer.

If you are a starter, you should know that Social Security does provide not only retirement benefits but also other programs like spousal benefits, children's benefits, disability benefits, and survival benefits, as well as supplemental benefits. However, you must meet the requirements, including age and disability status. You could qualify for more than one program.

Both residents and American citizens are eligible for Social Security benefits. You only need to provide the necessary documents in order to be approved. The approval process varies due to varying factors, which include the time taken to verify your documents by a Social Security administration officer. The approximate time is about six weeks. So, do not worry if you have applied, but you haven't received any response from them. I assure you they will respond to your application.

Reading this book will help you understand everything about Social Security and make better decisions.

Table of Contents

Introduction

Most people do not know the importance of social security in their lives and how it can also benefit their families, relatives, and kids. Established in 1935 as a part of the New Deal during the reign of President Franklin Delano Roosevelt, Social Security has continued to be a key component for a large number of Americans in their retirement, as well as old age. Both employers and employees in the United States pay into the system. It is believed that about 99% of the American workers will be absorbed into the system by the end of 2034. Without any doubt, the beneficiaries of Social Security are expected to have shoulder cuts before the deadline, and its future for the young population might be unclear if the government does not put a precise measure to run the program effectively.

Social Security, however, is facing four main problems. On June 2018, for example, statistics from Social Security Administration revealed that about 63.5 million Americans, of which two-thirds who have already retired, are now benefiting from Social Security. The average amount the government is spending on the retired workers per month is $1,348.49. The four problems include; rising life expectancies, congressional stalemate, a falling worker-to-beneficiary ratio, and near-record-low bond yields.

Despite all these serious problems, Social Security benefits have continued to provide monthly income for both married and unmarried Americans. Statistics show that about 71 percent of the unmarried old Americans and 48 percent of married Americans depend heavily on this Social Security Income. In other words, Social Security is the most critical program you should not miss to join in your life.

The Congress, however, has developed an interest in acting before the insolvency becomes a problem. The House of Representatives, for example, has received a proposal not only to lift the cap on the income subject to Social Security taxes but also increase the Social Security tax rates to be paid by all American workers and employees.

It is also essential to know that all employers in the United States have the specific responsibilities of paying their shares to the Social Security system regardless of the looming changes. As such, employers should understand all their responsibilities established in the Federal Insurance Contribution Act. The Federal Insurance Contributions Act, commonly known as FICA, is used to fund various social services, including social security and Medicare. These taxes are very regressive taxes since the rate is applied to every worker equally. To be precise, these taxes are not only withheld from workers' paychecks but also have no income exemptions or applicable deductions.

From our extensive experience, the FICA requires all employers to withhold Medicare taxes and social security from the wages of their employees. Just like employees, employers are supposed to pay a certain percentage of these taxes, and the amount must be the same as that paid by the employees. As an employee, for example, you are subjected to 0.9 percent Medical surtax only if you are earning over the amount determined in your tax filing status. According to Bill Goselin, an analyst for Paychex, all employers have a responsibility to report the wages of their employees on Form W-2. As an employer, however, you are supposed to fill the W-2s Form electronically if you are dealing with more than 250 forms and should also be filed with the SSA before the end of January 31.

Besides, FICA taxes are significant in the lives of retired workers. A study carried out to determine how American people have benefited from the FICA taxes shows that these taxes provide various benefits not only to the retired people and their beneficiaries but also to the disabled people.

We know that you may be wondering if your family can also benefit from your pension in case, you, as an employee, die. The most obvious answer is that your family will, without a doubt, benefit. Section seventeen of the Pension Act has clear guidelines on how your dependents, including your families and kids, can benefit upon your death or retirement. The condition is that you should have been worked in for at least five years. Some countries like Kenya and the United States require you to have worked for at least ten years for your family or children to enjoy these benefits.

Unfortunately, most of the employers in the United States do not know how to calculate their social security tax obligations correctly, even though the process is relatively easy. To effectively determine the amount you should be withholding from your compensations, you should take your gross wages and multiply with the tax rate (6.2%). This amount is what you should pay in the Social Security tax. Let us say that your gross wage is $100,000 per year. According to the current law, your employer should withhold 6.2 percent of your pay during that year, which is equal to $6200. The amount the employers contribute to the Social Security tax depends on the two main factors; their number of employees and the amount each employee earns per month or yearly.

There are many ways you can use to increase your credibility in any case of social security disability. It is essential to know that your credibility is the most important part of the social disability case, especially if you do not have severe disabling impairments like the one documented by the x-rays and MRIs. Many applicants rely heavily on their pain and other symptoms when they are showing the severity of their limitations. It is, therefore, essential to have an experienced DDS claim examiner to evaluate their initial applications. They should also have Administrative Law Judge (ALJ) not only for conducting hearing but also find their allegations believable, particularly if they are suffering from depression, fibromyalgia, or any other physical problems. The current Social Security regulations, however, require the ALJ to be present at your hearing to provide a clear picture of your credibility and the reasons for his/her findings. Do not worry about how you can increase your reliability.

Even though the future of Social Security is uncertain and undetermined, the government should, with immediate effect, take action towards reducing the risk associated with these programs. First, the government should work together with experienced and trusted financial advisors to come up with effective ways of investing and savings. This will help many American workers to achieve a comfortable retirement without necessarily depending on Social security as it is being witnessed at the moment.

Although there are other sources of income to retired people, Social Security has remained an important program in the United States. It saves a large population of Americans. Every eligible person receives a different amount of benefits from Social Security. In fact, the average wage depends on the worker's earnings and his/her full retirement age. For example, the percentage ranges will vary from seventy-five percent (75%) for the low-income earners, twenty-seven percent (27%) for the highest earners, and forty percent (40%) for medium earners. However, applying for earlier benefits will automatically lower these percentages, thus lowering your monthly Social Security benefits. You need to receive a monthly retirement benefit of about seventy percent for you to live a comfortable life after going for retirement.

Moreover, the current Social Security system allows you to work, and at the same time, pay your taxes into Social Security. In other words, you and your employers must pay part of your earnings to the system. The amount deducted, according to the current Social Security tax report, is twelve-point-one-five percent (12.15%). Social Security Administration pays benefits using tax money uses. People who can receive benefits include the retired, disabled, survivors, and dependents of the beneficiaries.

It is also important to know that the money we pay in taxes is not held in our personal accounts for us to use when we retire or apply for the benefits. Social Security uses our money to pay those who are already receiving the benefits. The unused money is then transferred automatically to Social Security trust funds. Most people, especially the young population, think that Social Security is just a program for the retired people in the United States. Yes, the majority of the people who receive benefits, according to Social Security's database, are old Americans. But it is good for you to know that the program provides financial help to any individual who meets their requirements. Although your age is also used to determine if you are eligible for Social Security benefit, there are some circumstances in which Social Security Administration does not consider it. The current Social Security statistic shows that children are the most beneficiaries of this program.

In terms of Medicare taxes, individuals are required to pay their Medicare taxes on all their wages, and those who are self-employed are supposed to pay from their net earnings. The amounts taxed on your earnings are used for your Medicare coverage.

Interestingly, Social Security uses 85% of your Social Security tax dollar to pay both the retired people and their families too. The amount is not only used to pay the surviving spouses but also children whose parents passed on while working. The remaining percentage, which is 15%, goes to a trust fund. The money is used to pay benefits to disabled people. In addition, the trust funds are used to ensure all Social Security programs are managed properly and with ease.

All people who enroll for Social Security are always provided with a unique Social Security number. The number is used by the Social Security administration to track your earning effectively, even if you are still working. Although Social Security provides its members with Social Security cards, it is important not to carry their cards everywhere. They need to be careful and should not give the card to anybody, even their friends or relatives. For example, various reports have revealed that most identity thieves are using other people's Social Security numbers to commit a crime; they can use your name to apply for more credits, especially if you have good credit.

It is also important to know that Social Security will, at any time, reveals your Social Security number to any person, including your spouse and children. However, it can only give your information to a person if you authorize them or law permits them to do so. Any person can contact Social Security any time if he/she needs a Social Security number, has lost his/her card, or would like to change his/her name on the current card.

For you to successfully apply for a Social Security card or replace your lost card, Social Security will not only ask you to complete a simple application but also provide copies of the required documents. The original copies of your documents are used for verification purposes. Social Security does not accept any photocopy or notarized document. You will not be asked to provide any proof of your citizenship or age when replacing the card. But those who are intending to change the name on their

Social Security cards are required to provide a document that shows that they have legally changed their names.

Generally, Social Security has emerged to be the best program in the United States as it reaches out to almost every family in the country. Not only Social Security helps the old Americans, but it also helps workers who have become disabled or got serious injuries while working. The 2018 Social Security's report indicates that about two hundred million Americans were working and paying Social Security taxes. Only sixty-two million people were eligible to receive monthly benefits.

Chapter One: Social Security

Introduction

For many years, Social Security has been one of the social insurance programs in the United States. A large number of American people rely on this program heavily for their retirements, survivor, or disability benefits. Statistics from the Social Security Administration (SSA) indicate that about sixty-five million Americans received one trillion American dollars ($1trillion) benefits in 2018. Developed to replace forty percent of the workers' income in retirements, the financial advisors believe that there is a need to have other sources of income like investments and personal savings as its alternatives.

The SSA has estimated that more than a third of the beneficiaries in the United States depends heavily on the Social Security benefits compared to their retirement income. The number is, however, likely to be affected either positively or negatively by various factors. These factors include a change in the demographics and the trustees of the social security trust fund or the surplus of funds.

This chapter provides a history of social security, the current state of Social Security, an uncertain future for Social Security, advantages of social security, and the problems Social Security is likely to face in the future.

History of Social Security

Enacted in 1935 during the reign of President Franklin D. Roosevelt, Social Security Act (SSA) led to the creation of social security to benefit both the disadvantaged and unemployed American people. Its main objective was to provide financial benefits to people who have retired and are over sixty-five years. The payment was made according to their payroll tax contributions. Without forget, it is good for you to know that the Social Security Board (SSB), which became Social Security Administration (SSA), was established by this Act not only to structure the Act but also to determine the best ways of implementing the Act.

The current statistics from the Social Security Administration show that through the SSA's inception, ten million Americans receive financial help every year. However, the program is still facing some challenges. The challenges are seen by many financial advisors as hot political topics and will continue to exist from time to time until we stabilize our political system. Without a doubt, the Social Security program was initially designed to enable employees to fund their benefits. Thousands of retired workers in the United States have already benefited from the system according to their earning history. In 1934, however, the government enacted two amendments to the Social Security program to enable both the survivors and the dependents of the workers also to enjoy social security benefits in case of death.

From 1934 to the 1950s, the social security program was virtually remained unchanged. It was from the 1950s when the American Congress decided to pass legislation that would offset the impacts of inflation. The legislation did not only increase the monthly benefits but also expanded Social Security to cover workers with disabilities. At that time, the government was running the Social Security program effectively.

In the 1970s, the program started experiencing financial stress as more people were being enrolled in it. The main factor that caused the system to experience the financial problem was the worsening of the economic conditions of the United States. The first short-term financial problem was witnessed in the 1980s. On trying to correct the situation, Ronald Reagan, a former American President, decided to appoint the Greenspan Commission. The commission was tasked with the responsibility of providing recommendations on how to change the legislation to address financial issues the program was experiencing. In 1983, the Greenspan Commission came up with several recommendations. The changes included increasing the retirement age to 67 and the introduction of the partial taxation of the benefits. These reforms were not only for solving the financial problems the program was facing but also to create a surplus fund.

The Current State of Social Security

Even though it is easy for you to fill out the form and collect your checks, there are some situations in which it may become challenging for you to start receiving the benefits. Some of the factors that can prevent you from receiving the benefits include income limitation, different rules, and age requirements.

Several changes that were made on Social Security in 1983 have to the growth of the program in the country. The retired workers or their dependents are nowadays expected to receive benefits on time. The SSA, however, estimates that the trust fund reserves will be exhausted by the end of 2037. You need to know that the Social Security Trust Fund continues to accumulate more funds than what it spends every year. Although the SSA expects the funds to maintain their surplus, change in demographics due to the reduced birth rates and longer lifespans in the country are the main factors for the depletion of the program's reserves.

If you do not know, Social Security is about pay-as-you-go. This means that every worker must pay to enable the currently retired workers to benefits. It is, however, unfortunate that the number of workers under retirements have reduced significantly in recent time. For example, the statistics show that the number of people reduced from four to two per retired beneficiary in 2017.

Since the continuing taxes to pay about seventy percent of the scheduled benefits, it will be better for the U.S Congress to make some changes to both the planned benefits and revenue resources. The changes should focus on making the program operate without experiencing financial stress, just like what was witnessed in the 1970s. Generally, Social Security continues to provide benefits to thousands of people. The program is financed through payroll taxes from employers and employees. Congress should also make sure that it continues to shape the program in the future to meet the needs of every generation.

The Future Status of Social Security

Recently, Social Security has been experiencing various threats and funding issues. The SSA believes that the program is facing long-term insolvency issues. According to the Social Security Administration, the program could experience a significant challenge if Congress does not immediately enact new legislation to reform it. To be precise, it may experience increased taxes and decreased benefits or forced to borrow from other government departments.

It is essential to know that the Social Security program is not expected to disappear entirely in the future. But, the SSA states that its benefits will reduce to about three-quarters of what was promised to the retirees. For example, those retired workers expecting to get $2,500 every month will receive $1,925 in the Social Security benefits.

Although the future of this program is uncertain, having a solid retirement plan is very important as it considers both the unknown and known factors. The SSA believes that people planning for retirements should take necessary steps to offset the problems associated with these programs to reduce the benefits. You should, therefore, work together with trusted financial experts to help you develop an effective strategy for savings and investing. This will help you enjoy a comfortable retirement.

Problems Facing Social Security

The current statistic from the SSA shows that about 60.4 million American workers, of which two-thirds are retired workers, benefit from the program. The average amount being spent on retired workers per month is $1,348.49, and the number is expected to increase in the next two years. Unfortunately, the program is likely to use its cash reserves at the beginning of 2020 excessively. This is, however, a terrifying forecast for those people who are heading into their retirements or have a little amount in the savings. Four main factors would make the Social Security program to collapse in the future. These factors include; fall in the worker-to-beneficiary ratio, rise in the life expectancies, near-record-low bond yields, and congressional stalemate.

a) The rise in the life expectancies

Several studies have revealed that life expectancy is one of the demographic factors that affect the operation of Social Security. In the 1960s, for example, an average adult had a life expectancy of 70 years but changed to 78.8 years by 2010s. Such improvement in life expectancy is caused by factors such as improved health education and improved medical care, among others.

During the designing of Social Security, the developers did not put into consideration that life expectancies can improve.

Instead, they thought that life expectancies would only reduce due to the reduction of various resources. It is, therefore, unfortunate that most people are now living longer. As such, they can benefits from social security payments for a longer time.

b) Fall in the worker-to-beneficiary ratio

Commonly known as the retirement of baby boomers, a fall in the number of workers to that of beneficiaries is the main problem facing social security in the United States. It is estimated that more than seventy million baby boomers are expected to join the retirement from 2010 to 2030, according to the SSA report. This means that a large number of people will be eligible to benefit from the project.

Unfortunately, those who developed Social Security did not predict that there would be such an increase in birth rates in the future. Even though many people are expected to go for retirement in the next five years, there are no enough people to replace them. For example, it is forecasted that the number of workers to the beneficiaries will fall to one from two-point-eight between 2020 and 2035. This shows that there we are likely to witness a low number of payroll tax revenue to support a large number of people who will be benefiting from the Social Security benefits.

c) Congressional stalemate

Even though congressional stalemate is another issue affecting Social Security, Congress has not taken any step to address this problem. There are various factors that are making it hard for the U.S Congress to enact laws that can satisfy the needs of workers and Social Security beneficiaries.

d) Near-record-low bond yields

It is essential to know that near-record-low rates do not only allow homeowners to refinance their mortgages, but also to buy homes with low mortgage rates. You can also expand or hire or even make acquisitions at a low cost.

Several studies have shown that low-interest rates have opposite impacts not only on the people but also on the funds coming from the fixed income assets. It is, therefore, essential for you to invest specifically in special-issue bonds that are only available to Trust funds. Note that a low yield does not affect the inflation rate.

Furthermore, most people think that it easy to start receiving benefits from the program once they are retired. From my experience, whether you are eligible to start receiving benefits, it is not as simple as filling out a form or collecting checks. Why is the process difficult than we think? The reason is simple. There are many different rules, income limitations, age requirements, and cut-offs that makes it hard for a person to receive the benefits. Also, Congress has continued to keep cutting back the budget, staff, hours, and whole offices. Combine that with the complexity factor. All these rules can, in fact, drive a person mad.

Most people think that American people are the richest people in the world. But this is not true. Whether you believe it or not, Americans are also more impoverished than they pretend. They do not even know how much they are giving up. Statistics show that only about three percent of the American population wait until they are seventy years old to start claiming. Surprisingly, the figures show a dramatic with a peak difference of 76% over claims at 62, especially when the most critical group files for the least amount offered. About half of the Americans cannot afford to postpone Social Security.

Misconceptions and Myths about Social Security Benefits

Social Security, as a topic, is fraught with misconceptions and myths that prevent some individuals from collecting their benefits. However, this is not true. Social Security has significantly changed the lives of many people across the world. Whether young or older, you can be eligible for Social Security and thus receive your social security benefits every month. The amount you receive is determined by your earnings history. The following are the myths about Social Security benefits:

The first myth about Social Security is that it is better for you to start receiving your benefits as early as possible. We have seen that you can collect your benefits as early as age 62. However, we do not advise you to do so, because this could lead to a permanent decrease in the amount of your monthly social security benefits. Under the current law, for instance, you will receive only seventy-five percent of your money. So, it is better for you to wait until you reach your normal retirement age, which is currently sixty-six (66). You can also receive more benefits if you wait until you turn seventy.

The second myth is that individuals can lose their benefits if they continue working. It is true that your benefit may reduce by one dollar for every two dollars of your income obtained above a certain threshold, which is currently $17,640. According to the Social Security Administration, the reduction of the amount of money received will continue to reduce until an individual reaches normal retirement age. You are entitled to earn as much as you want after reaching your normal retirement age. In fact, no reduction will be applied to your earnings.

There is also a myth that an individual cannot earn social security credits after reaching full retirement age. As a worker in the United States, you are likely to be bound to the Federal Insurance Contributions Act. However, the Social Security Administration does not depend on the amount of money deducted by the FICA; it will recalculate your primary insurance amount every year. It will credit you with one of your thirty-five highest indexed-earnings years after you start getting the benefit.

Another myth is that social security benefit is not taxed. A large percentage of people do not know that their benefits are also taxed if their earnings exceed a certain amount. Currently, Social Security requires you and your partner to pay income tax up to fifty percent of your benefits if you are filing a joint tax return. You will have to be taxed about eighty-five percent of your benefits if your combined income is above $44,000. In this case, combined income refers to the adjusted gross income and any non-taxable interest.

Lastly, there is also a myth that inflation can erode your social security benefits. Normally, this happens to those people who do not understand how COLA works. To be precise, COLA plays a significant part, as it is a key-planning booster for all beneficiaries.

In summary, different people were living a poor life to the extent that they could not afford to stand the uncertainties that were brought on by the disability, old age, death, illness, and unemployment in our lives. To reduce the poverty level, the Congress passed a Social Security Act in 1935. Since its establishment, Social Security has been providing benefits to retired people, disabled people, and their families. This has significantly reduced the level of poverty, not only in the United States but also across the world. It is, therefore, important to take this opportunity.

Chapter Two: Getting Started

Introduction

Before we look at how you can apply and get started, it is essential to know the importance of understanding your benefits when you join the Social Security program. The Social Security Administration estimates that social security benefits will make up to 39% of the Americans' income by the end of 2022. This will be for people aged between 65 and above. However, most workers, without knowing, find themselves making a decision that makes them miss hundreds of dollars once they get retired. If you are a beginner and would like to join the program, do not rush because you have seen most people, your friends, or workmates joining the program. The best thing to do is to understand how the system works and how you can benefit from it.

Applying for Social Security

If you are a starter, it is very easy for you to apply for your Social Security benefits. The process is very straightforward. The most important thing you should put into your mind before applying to join the program is to determine the best time to do so to enable you to receive the maximum amount of money in your retirement.

You need to know that Social Security can play a significant part in your retirement if you have a good plan since various studies show that the majority of older Americans live a long time. In other words, social security continues to play a vital role in preventing and reducing poverty in the United States. If you are wondering where and how to start applying for Social Security benefits, then the following six steps will help you get started.

Step One: Make the Right Decision

Most people in the United States find themselves applying for the Social Security program. They do not have a solid reason why they are applying for the program. Making a sound decision is very important in your life. There are other alternatives to Social Security that could help you achieve your objectives in life. Some people are not members of Social Security but are living a better life. So, it is important for you to make the best decision before joining the program.

Step Two: Check at your eligibility

Before you apply for Social Security, you should take your time to check if you are eligible. For you to be accepted to be a member of Social Security, you need to have worked for at least ten years and be at least 61 years and 9 months old. This has enabled 96% of the American workers to enjoy Social Security benefits.

Step Three: Understand Application Rules

Every system is governed by certain rules. You have to accept or adhere to those rules in order to be accepted as a member. Similarly, Social Security requires you to apply for the benefits four months before your Social Security paycheck is released to you.

Step Four: Gathering Personal Information and Documents

For starters, this step is the most tiresome among the six steps since it involves many things. But do not worry. The instructions provided in this step are straightforward. You need to have all the information and necessary documents to help you fill in the application. The information needed includes; your social security number, date of birth, and place of your birth.

But you must provide your permanent resident card number if you are not a U.S citizen. Other things to provide include; the name of your current spouse or any prior spouse. You can also get help from the SSA when it comes to determining whether including their benefits will increase your paychecks.

In addition to providing your residential card number, you will be required to provide the names and birth dates of your children, particularly those who became disabled under the age of 22 years or before getting married. The application also requires you to give the names and dates of your children aged between 18 to 19 years and are still in secondary school.

The next thing to do in this step is to provide details information about your current employment, employer, and other jobs you have held within the last two-to-three years. All this information is available on your Social Security statement online. You only need to have the name of your employer and the date you started working. But what if you are self-employed? It is very simple. You only need to provide information about the type of your total net income and the type of business you are operating. Moreover, you will need to provide the type of bank account, account number, and bank routing number if you decide to make a direct deposit (of social security benefits) into the bank account. For those without U.S bank account need to have bank name, currency type, transit number, the branch, bank code, and the bank country to facilitate the deposit.

Step Five: Completing the Application

Having the above-listed information makes the process of application easier than you are thinking. With this information, you will take about fifteen minutes to complete the whole application online.

Step Six: Reviewing and submitting your application

Lastly, you need to review your application before submitting it. It is important to know that the SSA will contact you in case they need you to provide them with some further information or have questions about the information you have provided to them. The applicants can also check the status of their applications on the internet at any time anywhere.

Online Application of Social Security

The introduction of modern technology has made it easy for people to apply for Social Security. You can apply it online using your personal computer, smartphone, or laptop at any time everywhere. The only thing you need is a stable internet. While applying over the internet, you will be asked to answer several questions about yourself, family, and work. Although the process is simple and straightforward, it is not a must for you to start and complete the whole application in one session.

The system was developed in the manner to stop at various points to allow you to confirm and save the information you have entered. As such, you can retrieve or continue with your application later safely. This is also important for you if, for example, you need to obtain some information you may be lacking at that particular time. The system also allows applicants to go back and make some changes or even fix errors before submitting their applications.

For you are among the starters who do not know the documents that are needed for them to start applying for Social Security online, then do not worry. The system has made it simple and easy for you. It will tell you all types of documents and information you need to provide for you to apply for the program successfully. You can decide to email the documents according to the instructions provided by the system or take them physically to any of the Social Security offices.

The last step is to sign the application. This is done electronically by pushing the button. A receipt with a confirmation number is then generated electronically to show you that you are done with the application. After receiving the receipt, you can confirm your application status later over the internet ant any place using your smartphone or laptop.

We advise you to make sure that you are using a secure network when you are filling out your form online, as this helps in preventing fraud, any snooping, or hackers from using your data for their personal benefits. Therefore, do not enter your Social Security numbers over an open network like the one provided by the hotels and coffee shops.

Unfortunately, most people do not know if the networks they are using are secure or not. Let us give you a hint to determine if you are using a secure network. Using a home network that requires you or any person to have a password to use it is fairly safe for you. But your network will be much secure if you use some security software. The software should include a firewall or guards to protect your computer against viruses or malware. You can also boost the security of your data by avoiding using a public network.

Advantages of Applying for Social Security Benefits on the Web

The introduction of the internet and modern technology came with its advantages and disadvantages. In our case, it is very convenient to apply for social security online. It does not only help you avoid some unnecessary trips to the nearest Social Security office, but also allows you to complete your application on time or even at your desired time.

According to the Social Security Administration, an applicant should take between ten-to-twenty minutes to complete their application online. There are other reasons why you should consider using an online application. First, the process allows you to correct or fix any errors before submitting the application. As an applicant, you can decide to go back at any time and correct any mistake made. The system provides you with an opportunity to review all your answers or make corrections before submitting the application for approval. Lastly, with the online application, applicants are sure that their applications have been received and are being reviewed since the system provides them with the receipts once they are through with their applications. As an applicant, you only need to print and keep the receipt, and then wait for approval of your application. The confirmation number helps you to follow your application status online. You can find this number on your receipt.

Advantages of Social Security

● Social Security provides monthly income to those in need of it

The current statistics from the Social Security Administration indicate that 85 percent of the funds paid into the system are distributed to both the qualifying individuals and retired workers. This shows that those people who would want to have monthly income after retirement have a chance to have it. The program provides supplemental income to help the retired workers and their children or families to maintain their living standards and lifestyle too.

● Provides a variety of benefits

Do you know that you can start claiming the benefits even when you are 62 years old? The only thing you are supposed to do in this case is to ask for retirements before claiming for the benefits. At that point, however, you will get a smaller payment per month when compared to someone who has waited to collect the benefits after reaching full retirement age. The secret of getting maximum benefits is claiming the benefits after turning 70 years. In fact, the structure is flexible and efficient for every person as you have the freedom to choose the structure that will work best for you.

● The ability to provide minimums for the individuals who have qualified

The Social Security Administration (SSA) came up with an alternative method in 1973 to calculate the benefits of those workers who are earning a low income. However, in 2018, eleven years of coverage provided a special minimum amount for primary insurance to be just $40.80. The special minimum coverage was $848.80 before 2018.

● Ability to all the spouses and children to collect the benefits

Most people think that Social Security is for working-class people. Yes, it was initially designed to reward those who were in the workforce. But nowadays, non-working people are also eligible for the benefits. However, the current rules allow non-working spouses to collect the amount, which is equal to fifty percent of their working benefits. They only need to have a minimum of twelve months in marriage at the time of submitting their application.

● Social Security provides benefits that are tax-free.

With the current laws, an individual in the United States is not allowed to pay an income tax to the federal government that is more than eight-five percent of their social security benefits. For example, you should expect that fifty percent of your benefits will be subjected to income tax if you file a joint return, or your combined income is about $32,000.

● Allows individuals to work during their retirements

The best thing with the Social Security program is that a person earns a larger benefit if he/she continues to work during his/her retirement. You can earn, in fact, keep on earning credits to your benefits if it is required. It is also important to know that working for a long time can delay your need to claim Social Security, and as such, increasing your benefits.

● Social Security is a long-time income

The most important thing with this program that you will be sure of a monthly benefit throughout your life once the SSA approves your application. Do not let your future life to be difficult. Whether you request for early retirement, you will still receive your benefits every month, though in smaller amounts than you could have received when you request at 70 years.

Disadvantages of Social Security

✓ Social Security is not funded fully

Several studies have shown that the number of people who are likely to benefit from Social Security is likely to increase by forty percent by the end of 2028. Some financial experts claim that this is even likely to take place as early as 2023. Also, high tax rates, federal deficit, and other financial stress are likely to affect the operation of the program.

✓ The system does not cover every person

Unlike it used to be when Social Security was established in 1935, the current system requires you to earn credits in order to qualify for the benefits. The minimum amount of credits you need to earn is forty (40) to be allowed to get a retirement benefit. But there is one way you can use to avoid this problem, which is to work more time to get more credit. The credit should be applied to your account. Moreover, 2018 rules require you to have earned a minimum of $5,280 for a period of twelve months with maximum credits of four in order to be allowed to enjoy the benefits. This means that it will take you ten years to qualify for this program if you are earning $5,280 per month.

✓ Social Security rewards those who earn more (high-income earners)

Truly, the system calculates your benefits according to the average amount of income you have deposited during the time you were working. Also, additional credits do not add value to your benefits once you have met the minimum amount of credits required for you to start receiving benefits. For example, the current equation for calculating monthly benefit is; 90% for the first $896, 32% for the amount from $897 to $5,399, and 15% for the amount that is above $5,399. Unfortunately, the current statistic shows that the majority of American workers earn below $5,399 per month, and thus, do not reach 15% calculation.

✓ Social Security is usually offered when it is difficult to enjoy or use its benefits

Various studies show that our health issues increase as we age. With Social Security, however, one has to delay the claim in order to earn maximum benefits. Most people are not enjoying as they would want since they are facing various health issues. From our experience, therefore, we would advise you to take the available benefits even if they are lower to enjoy your life. Larger benefits would help you to handle some major health problems in case you experience them as you age.

✔ High chance of changing Retirement Age

Since its establishment, Social Security has experienced some major changes in terms of law and its operation. This is because the current generation of people does not have lifespan and lifestyles as the generation of 1935. The full retirement age for those who were born between 1943 to1954 according to the Social Security Administration, is about 66, while those born is sixty-five. All people born in 1960 or later have a retirement age of 67. From this statistic, it is obvious that the retirement age continues to go up every year.

In general, it is easy for you to apply for Social Security online, as it will take you about ten-to-fifteen minutes. Although the approval period depends on how long Social Security will take to verify your documents, the process takes about six weeks in most cases. Also, understanding the advantages and disadvantages of Social Security is very important for you as it will help you determine whether to join the system. Make sure you understand the structure and the working of the system. Do not apply to join the system if you are not sure of your eligibility.

Chapter Three: Retirement Age and How to Qualify for Retirement Benefits

Introduction

Not every person who applies for retirement benefits gets it. There are many things Social Security Administration (SSA) considers to approve or decline people's applications. It is important for you to know that social security retirement benefit is governed by specific laws that concentrate on members' earning, particularly during their careers. According to the SSA, applicants need to have gained at least forty credits, which is equivalent to ten years of working, to qualify for the retirement benefits. Also, they need to have thirty-five years with their highest-earning to account for their benefit levels.

Meeting these requirements allows an applicant to start collecting the retirement benefits with the age of sixty-two years. However, those who wait until seventy years collect more benefits than collecting when you are only 62 years. Social Security believes that you will be in your full retirement age after attaining 62 years and above. This age allows you to collect the exact amount of money calculated by Social Security in accordance with your earning history. Also, a person cannot be penalized when he/she reaches that age (62 to 70 years).

Do you know that retirement age continues to change from time to time? Initially, all members were said to have attained full retirement age after reaching sixty-five years (65). But, the presence of funding crises witnessed by Social Security in 1983 made the congress to enact a new law to increase the retirement age. This was arrived at as a part of improving the operation of the program. That change means that nowadays, our social Security retirement age depends on the year in which we were born. This chapter will focus on attaining 62 years and earning Social Security Credit as the main factor that can make you eligible for full retirement benefits.

Attaining Sixty-Two Years to get Social Security
One of the requirements for you to be eligible for a retirement benefit is having 62 years. According to Social Security, you will not be entitled to any retirement benefits if you have not reached 62 years. However, there are some situations, which can make you start getting social benefit even before you reach 62 years. We will look at those situations later in this chapter. According to Social Security Administration, most American people qualifying for social security retirement benefits have the freedom to apply for retirement benefits as early as age 62 or at the age of 70 from the time they were born. Even though they have all these options, those who collect their retirement benefits get less monthly income. So, the best way to get maximum benefit is to wait until you reach 70 years.

Now, let us see the number of American people who collect or file for Social security at the age of sixty-two. Statistics from the Center for Retirement Research, which is based at the Boston College, indicates that about 70% of the Americans collect their Social Security benefits at the age of 62, and women are leading with 48%.

However, the current laws impose a penalty for those who apply for early Social Security. Some people receive this penalty as a surprise because early retirement leads to permanent reduction of your benefits. You should, therefore, know that claiming for early retirement benefits from Social Security attract the following percentages permanently on your Social Security; 5/9% per month when you apply 36 months before reaching age 62, and 5/12% per month when you apply beyond 36 months. For example, your benefit will be lower by 25% if you claim Social Security at the age of 62, and your full retirement age is 66. So, it is important to have comprehensive information about this penalty before you apply for early retirement benefits.

Getting Social Security Benefits before Turning 62
Do you know that a large number of Americans get their Social Security benefits before even turning sixty-two? The current statistic from the Social Security Administration (SSA) reveals that millions of American workers depend on Social Security benefits. Most of the American workers heading for retirements or want to end their careers, according to the SSA statistic, apply

for retirement benefits once they turn 62. This enables them to start getting their monthly retirement checks as early as possible.

Unfortunately, the majority of Americans do not know that they can get social security benefits even if they have not turned age 62. There are four main reasons that can make you be eligible for early application. The first reason is that you should be eligible for disability benefits. According to SSA, any American worker has the right to access disability benefits. However, you can claim these benefits only if you have accumulated enough work history. Another reason that can make sure to qualify for the disability benefits is your ability to show your inability to work due to medical conditions. Such medical conditions should be among those SSA considers as a disability. Upon successful demonstration, you will continue to enjoy these benefits until you gain your fitness to work on a regular basis.

Another reason that can make you qualify to get Social Security benefit is to show that you are an unmarried child with 18 years and below. The current Social Security laws allow unmarried children with 18 years and below to benefit from the program according to the working records of their parents. Those in high schools should be between 18 and 19, and their parents need to be receiving the benefits. Since the majority of parents in the United States, according to the statistics from the federal government, do not have minor children, these benefits are seen as disability benefits.

Another factor that can make you qualify for Social Security without necessarily looking at your age and work history is being married to any recipient of Social Security, and you are taking care of a child who qualifies for Social Security benefits. Do not, however, think that it is obvious that taking care of children who qualify for the benefits entitled you to enjoy Social Security. Under this provision, you need to prove that the child you are taking care of is not only receiving the benefits but is also 16 years or below. It is also important for you to know that this provision also gives advantages to divorced spouses. They can benefit from Social Security, especially if the children of their ex-spouses, who are disabled or aged below 16, are receiving Social Security benefits.

Normal Retirement Age

We have discussed both in our previous chapters, and in this chapter that those applying to get Social Security benefits can be approved only if they have a minimum of sixty-two (62) years. Commonly called "normal retirement age" in most parts of the world, "full retirement age" refers to the age a person must turn in order to start receiving social security benefits.

The normal age for retirement benefits ranges from age 65 for those people who were born before 1938 to age 67 for those applicants born in or after 1960. You also need to know that being a fully insured worker will give you an opportunity to earn retirement benefits in full at your normal retirement age. But the benefit will reduce only if you decide to apply for retirement as early as age 62. We hope that by looking at the table below, which shows the entire schedule for normal social security retirement age, will help you make a solid decision when it comes to applying for your retirement benefits.

Normal Social Security Retirement Ages Table

Birth Year	Normal Retirement Age
1937 and Prior	65
1942	65 and 2 months
1943 to 1954	66
1956	66 and 4 months
1958	66 and 10 months
1959	66 and 11months
1960 and above	67

Late Retirement

According to Social Security Administration, you can get maximum benefits from Social Security if your Social Security retirement is age 70. However, this does not mean that you should postpone your retirement past your normal retirement age. Late retirement has its negative impacts on the applicant. With the current social security laws, waiting for late retirement does attract not only permanent increases in the compensation amount within a short period but also encourages aged workers to work on a full-time basis. Truly, it is not a grant that you will get your retirement credit after passing your normal retirement age.

Retirement Earnings Test

Most people do not know that claiming their Social Security benefits before their full retirement age leads to a permanent reduction of their monthly benefits. It is, therefore, important for you to know that Social Security has two separate earnings thresholds. The first threshold, also known as the lower threshold, is applied to those people who cannot attain their full retirement age throughout the year. For example, $17,640 is the current lower-earning threshold.

On the other hand, the higher threshold is applied only to those beneficiaries who are able to attain full retirement age during the year. $46,920 is the current value. The best thing with this is that your benefits will not be subjected to withholding once you attain your full retirement age.

Disability Benefits

Disability benefit is given to those workers who cannot perform their normal work because of either mental or physical impairment. Such mental or physical impairment should take at least twelve months or can result in death. However, there are some situations in which you can stop receiving disability benefits.

How to stop Disability Benefits

Most of the American workers do not know that disability benefits can be stopped at any time if they do not meet the set requirements. The main reason why you may stop receiving your disability benefits under local and federal law or from your compensation is if you stop participating in rehabilitation. The 2018 Trustees Report revealed that about 850,000 American people receive their monthly benefits either because of the disabilities of their children or they are disabled. The most affected people are men, as women are only about $25,000.

How to Earn Social Security Credits

By working and paying social security taxes, a person gets to earn his/her social security credits. In simple terms, Social Security credits are the main factor that not only determines if a person is eligible to receive Social Security benefits, but also the number of benefits you will be receiving every month throughout your retirement. However, the number of credits needed to qualify for disability benefits or retirement benefits varies from one person to another since every person has a different normal retirement age.

Moreover, you can earn Social Security credits even if you are self-employed. In such a case, the amount of credit you earn can be adjusted every year in accordance with wage inflation. In 2018, for example, a worker received one credit if he/she was earning $1,130 each month.

Sometimes people use the terms "quarters of coverage" to refer to credits. This is because a person can earn a maximum of 4% every year. It is not a must for you to work throughout the year for you to earn a maximum of four credits per year. In 2018, for example, a person could earn four credits if he/she earned $4,520 or above in January and does not work for the rest of the year. So, you need to work smart in order to get the maximum credits per year.

Understanding How Social Security Works

Before you set your target to earn maximum credits per year, it is important for you to know how these credits not only work but also help you can maximize your monthly Social Security benefits. First, work credits refer to the measuring stick used by SSA to determine whether you have qualified for the Social Security benefits. You need to have a minimum of forty work credits to start receiving Social Security retirement benefits. Note that you must earn $1,300 to get one credit according to the law enacted in 2017 by the Social Security Administration.

In general, it is easy for you to receive Social Security retirement benefits if you meet all the requirements. First, you need to have a minimum of forty (40) credits and attained a minimum age of 62. However, you are allowed to wait until you turn 70 years to apply for Social Security benefits. This will help you receive maximum Social Security benefits. Also, late retirement attracts some permanent benefits. In this case, the amount you receive per month will depend on the amount you have been paying throughout your working.

Chapter Four: Calculating Retirement Benefits

Introduction

In our previous discussions, we have seen that there are various factors that determine your eligibility for Social Security Retirement benefits. These factors include; (1) attaining a minimum of 40 social security credits and (2) having 62 years or above with 35 years of working. In this chapter, however, we are going to look at how you can calculate your Social Security retirement benefits.

It is important to ask yourself about the amount you will be getting from Social Security before making a plan for your retirement. Various researches show that most American workers request their retirement benefits at the age of 62. This makes them receive a minimum amount of benefits from Social Security. You need to use the retirement estimator to find out the exact amount you will be receiving when you apply for your retirement benefits. The estimator is found online. Workers with the age of 18 years and above can apply for these benefits online. They only need to create their accounts before requesting their social statements.

A large number of American populations do not know how to determine their retirement benefits, according to the Social Security Administration (SSA). Our retirement benefits are calculated based on our lifetime earnings. The SSA can decide to adjust or index our actual earnings to our accounts. Lastly, retirement benefits are one of the components that everyone wishes to have as they age. In fact, financial experts see it as a source of income that helps workers during savings. Workers are able to determine the amount of money they will be saving every month in order to live a better future life.

Appropriate Time to Collect Your Social Security Benefits

You cannot collect your retirement benefits if you have not reached the time set by the Social Security Administration. This is because your social security benefits are calculated in accordance with your working history. The SSA assumes that all workers take their retirement at their normal retirement age, which depends on the year their date of birth. According to the Social Security database, the full retirement age (FRA) is not the same for every member. For example, the retirement age of people born in 1937 or earlier is not the same as those people who were born from 1955 to 1959. The FRA for 1937 and 1955 are 65 and 66, respectively. To be precise, the FRA has been increasing with time, and it is estimated that it may be more than 70 by 2032.

Moreover, retired workers have the freedom to file their retirement immediately; they turn 62 or wait until they turn 70. The two options have their own advantages and disadvantages. Filing your retirement as early as possible is not the best option, even though many American workers prefer this option. You will get minimum benefits when compared to a person who requests the retirement benefits at the age of 70. Essentially, delay or early retirement impacts the amount of money you receive per month. For example, going for early retirement means that you will be receiving lower monthly benefits while delay retirement provides you to maximize your monthly social security benefits. Even though retirement benefit increases every year during the retirement period, it is important to know that the increase depends on the history of your earnings. As such, it is obvious that our future benefits can reduce when we decide to go for early retirement benefits. Therefore, the best time to collect your benefits is waiting until you reach 70 years if you want to gain maximum social security retirement benefits.

Do you decide the Amount of benefit to Pay Out?
Although Social Security allows you to decide the time to start receiving your benefits, the time to select must be between sixty-two and age seventy years, according to the current social security law. It is the government that determines the amount to pay each recipient. After initiating the process of claiming your benefits, Social Security will start paying you the same amount of benefit each month. The amount you will be receiving will depend on two main factors; your lifetime earnings records and your age (the time you started claiming the benefits). However, you cannot decide to increase the amount to withdraw to cater for your expenses.

Additionally, you cannot claim your retirement benefits at the age of forty, even if you are feeling ill. However, you may qualify for disability benefits depending on the condition of the disease. Although an individual can still cash out his/her private retirement accounts without someone approving it, this will attract a penalty.

Calculating Social Security Benefits

Before the introduction of advanced technologies, it was very hard for American workers to calculate their Social Security benefits. However, after realizing how challenging it was, the Social Security Administration started concentrated on how to ease the process. The SSA finally came up with an online calculator to help workers calculate their benefits. Workers can use an online system or request help from Social Security by filing Form SSA-7004. The Form can be obtained directly from the SSA.

Moreover, using the retirement estimator available online provides workers with an estimate that contains an estimate of their benefits at their minimal and maximum normal full retirement ages and FRA. Using this estimator enables you to know that SSA contains various calculators like the quick calculator to help you plan your retirement properly.

Statistics from the federal government shows that Social Security has helped many American workers since it was established in 1935. Despite its famous, many people still do not know how to determine their retirement benefits even after introducing a retirement calculator online. We believe that having the ability to calculate your retirement benefits is very important to you as you will be able to know how much you will be receiving during your retirement. You can also use the knowledge to come up with proper saving plans, thus avoiding using the money on non-essential commodities or activities.

Steps for Calculating your Social Security Retirement Benefits

Step one that workers should use to calculate their social security benefits is by determining their AIME, commonly called average indexed monthly earnings. Social Security Administration, however, calculates your earning by taking your total earnings. Total earnings, in this case, refer to the amount you had earned when you started working. The formula being used determines workers' AIME by using their top thirty five earning years. You can calculate your Social Security benefits by getting the total amount of earnings of all your 35 years, and then divide it by thirty-five to determine your yearly average. Divide the annual average with twelve to get the number of benefits you will be getting every month throughout your retirement.

The next step is to calculate your PIA using your average indexed monthly earnings. You should know that the SSA uses indexed monthly earnings to determine the basic retirement benefits of the workers. Such benefits are called the primary insurance amount (PIA). The PIA and workers' current age when they were applying to Social Security is used to determine their initial social security benefit.

Use your average indexed monthly earning in the formula to find your PIA. In 2018, for example, the formula for determining PIA was; 90 percent for the first $895 in AIME, thirty two percent for the amount of AIME greater than $895, and fifteen percent for the amount greater than $5,397. It is important to know that these percentages remain the same every year. Your PIA depending on the bend points of your first year, is always eligible for social security according to the current Social Security Law, which also allows you to start receiving your social benefits after turning age 62.

Adding COLAs is the next step in calculating your Social Security benefits. We have seen that Social Security determines your PIA (primary insurance amount) by looking at your bend points at the time you are 62 years old. The PIA is always adjusted upward when a person makes a claim after turning 62. The level of adjustment depends on the given cost-of-living adjustments (COLA). For example, your monthly retirement benefits will increase by a certain figure if the COLA increases with a certain percentage.

While calculating your Social Security retirement benefits, it is important for you to consider if you need early or late retirement. Usually, the normal retirement age various in accordance with your time of birth. It can be 62, 66, or 67, or something else. For example, those claiming their Social

Security retirement benefits before they reach their full retirement age receive less monthly benefits when compared to those who apply late. This is because the amount calculated reduces by almost 0.56 percent every month for a period of 36 months. But applying when you have turned age 70 or reached your normal retirement age enables you to receive maximum monthly Social Security benefits. The benefits increase permanently at a rate of 8 percent per year.

Factors Contributing to Change in the Amount of Retirement Benefits

In the early discussions, we have learned that the amount of our retirement benefits is not the same for all people. The variations are caused by various factors, such as choosing to receive your benefits before or after your normal retirement age, your eligibility for cost-of-living benefits that start to increase once you turn 62, applying for social security benefits just past your normal full retirement age, and being a government worker who receives a pension. All these factors affect the amount of Social Security retirement benefits a person receives throughout his/her retirement period.

Effects of Earning Records on Your Retirement Benefits

We have seen that there are various factors that can affect the amount of your Social Security benefits. However, your earning history also called earned income, is the main factor that determines how the amount of social security retirement benefit you will be receiving every month when you turn your normal retirement age. According to the Social Security Administration (SSA), Social Security taxes are always taken out of workers' paychecks based on their earnings. The program allows you to receive your benefits even if you are still working. But in this case, you must have attained your retirement age. A worker can also decide to reduce or delay his/her Social Security benefits at any time.

Normally, our primary insurance amount (PIA) is determined according to our earning history, specifically on the AIME, which refers to average indexed monthly earnings. Previously, we have seen that PIA is the benefit you will receive when you decide to receive your retirement benefits at your normal retirement age. The AIME, on the other hand, is a calculation Social Security uses to determine the PIA. It takes into account the thirty-five years that exhibited your top earnings until you turned 60 years. From these explanations, it is evident that a person with a higher earning history will get more retirement benefits that those with low working history.

How to Calculate Average Indexed Monthly Earnings (AIME)

Before we look at how you can calculate your AIME, it is important to know that AIME plays a vital role in determining Social Security disability allowance. It is the figure that Social Security uses in calculating our Social Security disability allowance.

To determine your AIME, however, Social Security takes the total amount of your thirty-five highest years of earning, which can go up to age sixty and divides it by the number of months you have worked before turning age 60. In other words, use the following steps to calculate your AIME:

✔ First, obtain your Social Security Statement online and determine the amount of money that Social Security taxed from your earnings.

✔ Using the national wage-indexing factor, multiply it with your yearly taxable earning as this will help you obtain your adjusted earnings for each year.

✔ Then add all your adjusted earnings to determine the total amount of your adjusted earnings from the time you were 21 years old to disabled.

✔ Finally, take your total adjusted earnings and divide it with your working period.

The maximum amount you can get from your Social Security Retirement Benefit

Social Security operates under the laws, which must be signed by the president. Since its establishment, several laws have been enacted to control its operation. Such laws have made the system to experience many changes in its operation.

Statistics from Social Security Administration show that the maximum amount of Social Security benefits paid in 2018 at the normal retirement age is $2,861. However, a person can decide to increase this amount by a late retirement application. For example, if you retire and delay to claim your retirement benefits for two years that is beyond your FRA, you will receive a greater monthly benefit. To be precise, your monthly benefit will be 16 percent larger than PIA. This is obtained as follow; 2/3 x 24 = 16%. Therefore, your monthly benefit will increase from $1,400 to $1,624.

Let us find out the amount you will receive when you decide to claim your retirement benefits four years after retiring. In this case, you will receive a monthly benefit that is 32% more than your PIA. It is calculated as follow; (2/3 x 48) % = 32%. Therefore, your monthly benefits will increase permanently to $1,600 to $2,112.

Managing Social Security Money

Most people think that their contributions to Social Security go into their personal accounts. The money you contribute to Social Structure does not reflect in your individual names; instead, all Social Security contributions go into one collective pot. In fact, there is no way you will determine how Social Security should manage the money since the system works as an intergenerational wealth transfer. In other words, the money that we contribute to the system is used by the Social Security Administration to pay the current retirees.

Depending on various factors, including your retirement age, your marital status, and earnings records, you may end up receiving a better or worse monthly benefit on your investment. As such, some people prefer to invest in other government programs other than Social Security, especially if the programs have better returns.

In summary, many American workers enroll for Social Security benefits to avoid depending on their children, families, relatives, or the community. They all know that they will retire one day. Many governments, including the American government, believe that retirement is where an individual leave their work because their age cannot allow them to work as normal. This age is called the full retirement age, which is currently sixty-five. To determine the amount you will be receiving each month after attaining your full retirement age, Social Security Administration takes into consideration your lifetime earnings and the thirty-five years of your average earnings. Claiming your retirement benefits as early as age 62 can lead to a permanent reduction of your monthly benefits while late claiming can lead to an increase in your monthly benefits.

Lastly, the government plays a vital role in the success of the Social Security system. It allocates the necessary resources, enacts laws to determine how much each employer and employee must pay for Social Security, determine the amount each retired or disabled person will receive, and pass laws that prevent people from opting out of the system.

Chapter Five: Social Security

Medicare

Introduction

Many people in the United States do not know that the Social Security Administration provides medical information to workers to help them live a better life. However, one must have 65 years and above, receiving Social Security Disability benefits, or has permanent kidney failure to qualify for this program. This chapter provides comprehensive information about Medicare, how you can qualify for the medical program, and the options you can choose for Medicare coverage.

Medicare

Medicare plays an important part in the United States since it is a program that covers not only people aged sixty-five years and above but also covers young people with permanent kidney failure, amyotrophic lateral sclerosis, or certain disabilities that are specified. Although the program was established to cover the cost of health care, it does not cover all medical expenses. But the best part of it is that you can choose how you will be getting your Medicare coverage. In fact, Medicare coverage provides you with an opportunity to purchase a Medigap, which is a Medicare supplement policy that covers some of the medical costs that are not provided by Medicare. Such supplement policies are found in any private insurance company.

Now, let us see how this program works. A certain percentage of the amount you and your employer pay (payroll taxes) are used for covering most of your Medical expenses. Also, a monthly premium is deducted from your Social Security check to cover some medical costs.

Four Parts of Medicare

It is important to know that Medicare contains for parts, namely; hospital insurance, medical insurance, Medicare advantage, and Medicare prescription drug coverage. To start with, hospital insurance is used for paying inpatient care and skilled nursing facilities in the hospital. It also pays for both hospice care and home health care. Unlike hospital insurance, medical insurance is used to pay for the services doctors, and other health providers offer to you. Medical advantage deals with all benefits and services that are covered under hospital insurance and medical insurance. Lastly, Medicare prescription drug coverage will help you cover all the costs of prescription drugs.

Most people think that Medicare is the same as Medicaid. The two programs are totally different from each other. Medicaid is a program run by the state and provides both medical and hospital coverage to people earning a low income. Every state has its rules that not only reveal about your eligibility to join the program but also what the program covers. You can be eligible for both Medicaid and Medicare.

Qualifications for getting Medicare

According to the Social Security Administration, not every person is entitled to Social Security Medicare program. Before Lyndon Johnson, a former U.S President signed a law that led to the establishment of Medicare and Medicaid in 1965, the majority of American people aged sixty-five or even older were living without any insurance to cover their hospitalization. Most of them lacked plans to cover doctor visits. Sometimes older Americans with private medical insurance were removed from Medicare coverage by their companies. You should not worry nowadays if your insurance is terminated due to preexisting conditions.

There are certain requirements you must meet for you to qualify for Medicare. The requirements vary according to the type of Medicare you are applying for.

Requirements for Hospital Insurance

One of the requirements for you to be entitled to this type of Medicare is that you must be an American citizen or a permanent U.S resident with 65 years and above. The other requirements include:

✔ Must be eligible or receiving Social Security benefits,

✔ Must be receiving railroad social security benefits,

✔ Have a spouse receiving Social Security benefits. The spouse can be living, deceased, or even divorced.

✔ Have a long history of working in the government and shows that you have paid for Medicare taxes,

✔ Must be a dependent parent with a fully insured child who deceased.

Failure to meet the above requirements, however, cannot prevent you from getting hospital insurance. You can still get this Medicare if you pay a monthly premium, according to Social Security Administration.

Requirements for getting Medical Insurance

You need to know that any person who is eligible for hospital insurance can also enroll in medical insurance when he/she pays a monthly premium. Unlike hospital insurance, the amount you pay for medical insurance depends on your income. You will pay a higher monthly medical insurance premium if you are earning income.

Other factors that are considered for you to get medical insurance if you are not enrolled in hospital insurance include; be a U.S. citizen or a permanent U.S. resident who has been living in the country for at least 5 years.

Medicare Advantage Plans

This is another important part of Medicare. People who receive their medical and hospital insurances from the government have original Medicare. But those who receive their benefits from private companies have Medical Advantage plans if those companies are approved by Medicare. Most of the plans are good for you because of the minimal costs involved and their ability to provide extra coverage.

The best thing with Medicare Advantage plans is that they cover many things that are covered by the Medigap policy. As such, there is no need for you to take a Medigap policy. One of the benefits you will enjoy when you get Medicare Advantage plan includes providing you with extra days in the hospital. You will not pay for those days you spend in the hospital when getting treatments.

To join a Medicare Advantage plan, applicants must use their health cards, which are provided by the company offering Medicare Advantage plans. Apart from using health cards, they can join by paying monthly premiums for their plan due to its extra benefits.

Medicare Prescription Drug Coverage

This is the last part of Medicare a person can get according to Social Security Administration. You are still eligible for this program if you have either hospital insurance or medical insurance. It is not a must for you to join this plan; you only do it voluntarily. This plan attracts an extra monthly premium, and the amount to pay depends on your income. Late enrollment also has its penalty, which you must pay for once you have the coverage.

How do Low-Income People Pay Medicare

For low-income earners, it is easy to get help to pay their Medicare premiums. Normally, the state provides help to such people through various programs. For example, some programs pay Medicare premiums while others deal with Medicare deductibles. However, you need to have hospital insurance for you to join any of these programs. You should also prove that your income and resources are limited, thus not enough to pay Medicare.

It is only your state that has the ability to determine whether you qualify for any of these programs since each state has its rule. Feel free to contact your local medical assistance agency, the welfare office, or even social services to know if you qualify for these services.

Applying for Medicare

Many people in the United States do not know how to apply for Medicare even though they are receiving Social Security benefits or even railroad retirement checks. But those living in states, such as Washington, D.C., Guam, or American Samoa, have already joined Medicare without their knowledge. These states have special laws that require them to enroll their citizens into hospital insurance and medical insurance automatically. However, you should get in touch with Social Security three months before turning age 65 if you are not getting Social Security benefits. They will help you sign up successfully. There are also other situations that enable you to enroll for any of these programs. For example, you can contact Social Security to enroll you if you are; a widower with 50 to 65 years, government employee, and your kid has permanent kidney failure, among others.

Initial Enrollment Time for Medical Insurance

Some people do not understand the time frame for signing up for medical insurance after enrolling in hospital insurance. However, it is important to know that a person has a period of seven months to sign up for medical insurance after becoming eligible for hospital insurance. The seven-month period is known as your initial enrollment time. For example, the initial enrollment period of a person can start three months before turning 65 years if he is eligible at age 65. But those permanent kidney failures or any disabilities have different initial enrollment period as their period depends on the time their treatment or disability started.

Effective Medical Insurance

Your enrollment in medical insurance does not become an effective instant. Social Security will evaluate the information you have provided before deciding whether you are eligible for this part of Medicare. Those who enroll in the first three months of their initial enrollment period will have their coverage effective in the first month of their eligibility.

However, you should not worry when you miss enrolling in medical insurance during the initial enrollment period since Social Security provides people with the opportunity to enroll from January to March every year. This period is called the Special Medicare Enrollment Period.

Special Enrollment Period for Medicare

Many people find themselves not enrolling in Medicare because they did not find time to enroll within a regular period set up by Social Security. However, this should not prevent you from signing up in Medicare since there are some situations that allow an individual to enroll in Medicare even if the set time is over. However, you need to qualify for the Medicare Special Enrollment Period to be allowed to enroll in Medicare.

Having 65 years and above, as well as being covered by a group health plan, makes you eligible for a Special Enrollment Period (SEP). With SEP, you can go ahead and enroll in medical insurance, which is Medicare Part B. From this, it is obvious you can decide to delay your enrollment in hospital insurance without paying a 10 percent premium fine or wait for the general enrollment period. Statistic from Social Security shows that the majority of American workers receive medical insurance without paying monthly premiums since most of them have not only worked for at least ten years but also paid Medicare taxes.

Effects of Medicare on Our Health System

Several studies have shown that a large number of American workers nowadays get their private insurance while working. The situation is different from what was witnessed in 1965, where 50% of the aged Americans did not know about health insurance according to the Social Security report. The same report shows that 64% were couples, 37% were unmarried men, and 49% were unmarried women. During that time, the majority of Americans (elderly) depended on their children, avoided care, or looked for charity any time they needed medical services since most of them had spent their savings.

However, the amendment of Social Security, which was initiated in 1965 to curb the rapid number of elderly who were depending on their children, has positively impacted the lives of many people in the United States. The current Social Security's statistic shows that less than one percent of the elderly Americans neither have health insurance nor access to medical treatment. It has become the largest program in the United States that covers our health as it accounts for twenty percent (20%) healthcare expenditure. To be precise, the program has provided health insurance for disabled people, low-income people, and seniors.

Advantages of Enrolling in Medicare

Unlike other health programs in the United States, Medicare offers various services to American people, like helping them to live a better life. With this program, you can get various preventive and screening services without paying a single coin. For example, medical insurance, which is Medicare part B, provides free screenings for diseases like cervical, breast cancer, prostate cancer, and cardiovascular diseases.

Another advantage of Medicare is that it leads to better care for all people. According to the Social Security Administration, a Medicare program was established to ensure that people, including elderly and disabled people, get better health care. However, some amendments have been made to the program with the aim of improving the quality of health services to all people.

Medicare is also efficient when compared to private insurance in the United States. Various studies show that more American workers are enrolling in Medicare, with an increase of 1.4% from 2015 to 2018. The overall Medicare spending, however, is less than 5%. The program has been providing health coverage to more than nine million people with disabilities who were not approved to get private insurance. After its enactment in 1965, the lives of elderly Americans have improved a lot as this program cuts their poverty rate by half. It provides various health services to many people, including people with permanent kidney failure or with limited resources.

Enrolling Loved One in Medicare

Most people in the country do not know that Social Security allows them to enroll their loved ones in Social Security Medicare. It is important for you to make sure that your loved ones benefit from this program, as it has helped many people in the Country. Various researches have revealed that both young people and adults have a high possibility of suffering from chronic diseases. In fact, 80% of the people with 50 years and above are suffering from chronic disease, showing that the disease gets worse as we age.

Treating people suffering from any chronic conditions is costly. You need to have a lot of money in order to treat the conditions, something that is always hard to most people living in the country. But the establishment of the Medicare system has significantly helped many people suffering from any of chronic conditions since it provides a variety of care at nursing homes and hospitals. Now, let us see how you can help an elderly person or your loved one to enroll in Medicare.

You can help your loved one to enroll in Medicare by telling them about the importance of enrolling in the program. Some people, especially illiterate ones, do not know that this kind of program exists in the country. Help them to sign up in the program if they agree to join. The best way to convince them is by telling them how Medicare plays a large part when it comes to treating conditions such as chronic illness.

When to Enroll your Loved One in Medicare

After determining the best Medicare plan for them, you can proceed on with the process of enrollment to enable them to start receiving healthcare coverage. You can choose to enroll them during the four periods, namely, Initial Enrollment Period (IEP), General Enrollment Period (GEP), Open Enrollment Period (OEP), and Special Enrollment Period (SEP).

How your Loved Ones can pay for Medicare

We have seen that it is easy to pay for Medicare. You should know that the premium amount for your loved ones will come out of their Social Security checks. But you can tell them to contact Social Security Administration, either in-person or via phone if they are not members of Social Security.

To enroll your loved one in Medicare Advantage plans, they will have to pay for monthly premiums directly to the insurance company. However, it is your care doctor or any other specialist to directly bill your loved one for any costs that Medicare does not cover. But you can use supplemental plans to help your loved ones cover all the bills, which are not covered by Medicare. Such plans are usually provided in private insurance companies, and your loved one must pay a monthly premium to get them.

In summary, Medicare is a special social insurance program that has helped many people, not only in the United States but also across the world. The program currently provides medical coverage to more than eighteen million Americans. This has, however, put more pressure on the government to control health care spending. It has four main programs; hospital insurance benefits, medical insurance, Medicare Advantage, and Medicare Advantage prescription drug plans. Also, you should not only understand how all of these programs work but also their advantages and disadvantages when you sign up.

Chapter Six: Taxes and Social Security

Introduction

The majority of American populations, especially the youth, feel unhappy when Social Security taxes their incomes. Although 15 percent of your Social Security benefit is not taxed regardless of how much you earn per month according to Social Security Administration (SSA), the remaining amount of your income is taxed based on the amount of money you receive. Statistic from SSA shows that about forty percent of the people in the United States, who receive Social Security pay income taxes.

In addition, the majority of retired workers cannot depend only on Social Security for their treatments and survival. For example, the average person who receives Social Security benefits currently in the country gets just $1,420 per month. Also, the maximum amount of social benefits you can receive as Social Security benefits per month is $2,849. You need income from your investments or retirement savings accounts to live a better life.

The Taxation of Your Social Security

Before we look at how Social Security we carry out the process of taxation on your Social Security benefits, it is important to understand that provisional income refers to the sum of your adjusted gross income (AGI), non-taxable interest, and fifty percent of your annual Social Security benefits. This is represented as follow:

Provisional Income = Adjusted Gross Income (AGI) + Non-Taxable Interest +50% (Annual Social Security benefits).

You must know that no one is taxed by Social Security if his/her provisional income is $25,000 or less for a single filter. But things change if the provisional income for the joint filter is between $34,001 and $44,000. Social Security will tax 50 percent of your Social Security benefits.

Let us say, for example, that John, a retired man, gets Social Security benefits of $17,040 per year. He also receives $31,480 from other sources of his income every year. Using the above provisional formula, it is true that John has a provisional income of $40,000. According to SSA, 85% of his total Social Security benefit will be taxed at his marginal tax rate.

But you should not worry about this calculation, especially if you are not good at mathematics because SSA does send earning statements to all recipients of Social Security. The statement shows the amount they have received as benefits in the entire tax year. Moreover, the statement is used by the recipients to fill out their income tax returns to the federal. There are some situations where the recipients might pay their taxes on their benefits. The most common situation is if the recipients want to pay ahead of time. They are allowed to make an estimated payment.

Moreover, Social Security is not in good shape as it used to be between 1935 and 1965. During that time, all workers who had enrolled in the program used to get better healthcare since they were not as many as they are today. Currently, the program has over ten million people who receive Social Security benefits. The number is expected to double in the next two years. This is stressing the federal government financially.

Will you be taxed if Social Security is the Only Source of your Income?

It is good to know that Social Security will not tax your Social Security income because of various reasons. Some of these reasons include; the money you are collecting is not as a result of renting out the property, and you are no more working.

Having Other Sources of Income

The current Social Security law gives Social Security power to tax a certain portion of your Social Security benefits if they find out that you do receive income from other sources. Normally, the taxable position ranges from 50% to 85% of what you receive from Social Security benefits.

The Base Amount and its Working

We are going to use some examples to show you how the base amount works if you do not have an idea. Now let us say that John receives $15,000 per year as an investment income and continues to work at least one day every week. He earns $7,000 per year for only doing that work. He also collects $18,000 as Social Security retirement benefits, of which $9,000 is taxed every year.

Analyzing the above example, it is true that John's provisional income will be $31,000. You can calculate his provisional income (PI) using the formula we discussed earlier, which is; PI= Investment income + wages +Social Security benefits. Therefore, the provisional income, in this case, will be $15,000 plus $7,000 plus, which is equal to $31,000. His provisional income will be more than the threshold by $6,000 if he has a single filing status.

Possible Adjustments on the Base Amount

Surprisingly, in the above example, there is a possibility that John's Social Security benefits can be tax-free if his retirement benefit is only $7,500. Unfortunately, this will place John under the provisional income threshold of $25,000, even if he continues doing his part-time work. To get his provisional income, you will need to add his investment and Social Security benefits together. Social Security will apply the same to him, even if he decides to stop working part-time.

The good news is that all American workers or retired workers have the freedom to make some adjustments to their income if they decide to do so in advance. This depends on you. Using John as an example, John can make an adjustment to his income if he thinks that his benefits are going to place him against his PI threshold by giving up his one-day-a-week job. It is better for you to consult any tax professionals to help you understand your potential liability if you are having many sources of income in addition to your Social Security benefits. The expert will also help you know the exact amount of money you will be receiving after all taxes.

Rules about Married Couples

You must know that the same rules for the base amount and an additional amount will be applied to any person enrolled in Social Security if he/she is married and files a joint tax return. He/she will calculate the amount basing on his/her income, as well as Social Security benefits. His income thresholds will increases to $44,000 and $32,000 for the additional amount and provisional income, respectively.

However, married couples filing their tax returns separately enjoy various opportunities like reduced base amount when computing their Social Security benefits. But those living separately throughout the year from each other have an option of using $25,000 and $34,000 as base amount and additional income amount respectively since Social Security sees them as single.

Social Security Benefits Withholding

Many people think that federal income tax cannot be withheld from their Social Security benefits. This is wrong. Every person who is enrolled in Social Security und can decide to have his/her Social Security benefits withheld after realizing that he/she might pay to tax some of the benefits in the future. The specific rates at which federal income tax can be withheld in this year range from seven to twenty-two percent. All workers and retired workers are limited to this range, and no one can even opt for a flat dollar amount or another percentage. You can let the SSA know the amount you would like them to withhold from your Social Security benefits by filing Form W-4V.

States Taxing Social Security

Not all states in the United States tax Social Security benefits. Statistics show that about thirteen states impose taxes on Americans' Social Security benefits at the moment. Only thirty-seven states are the one, which does not tax benefits. Out of thirteen states, five use federal rules to determine the exact amount to tax your Social Security benefits while the remaining have their own rules.

Maximizing your Social Security Benefits

We have seen that there are some American workers or retired people who find themselves paying up to eighty-five percent of their Social Security benefits. Such rules on taxation differ from one state to another. They are not like the earned income rules, meaning that they do not to people who receive their benefits before their normal retirement age.

Social Security Tax Rates

The federal government requires employers to submit their employees' tax every month. The tax rate Social Security uses does not vary, no matter how much you earn. The current rate used by Social Security to tax both the employer and the employee as a single business is twelve percent. Every employer uses a rate of twelve percent. You will contribute half of the amount and your employer the remaining amount. To be precise, you only pay six percent but not twelve percent since you and your employer shares twelve percent equally.

Note that the tax is performed on all your sources of income, such as bonuses, salaries, and wages. $127,000 is the income limit if you are working for somebody. If you are self-employed, however, the IRS will view you as both an employer and employee. As such, you will be required to pay the whole social security tax.

Social Security Income Taxes for the Seniors

You may be wondering if seniors are also required to pay taxes on Social Security income. Truly, a large number of seniors in the United States get surprised when they realized that their Social Security benefits are subjected to taxes. You should know those retired people who are still working part-time are subjected to taxation. Part of their benefits is taxed if the amount is larger than the set income limits. However, you should know that no annual earnings limits will be applied to you after attaining your normal retirement age.

Minimizing or Avoiding Social Security Taxes

The 2018 report from Social Security shows the majority of American workers continue to pay into the social security programs even after attaining their normal retirement age. But do you know that there are ways you can use to avoid paying income tax on your Social Security benefit? It is very easy. Social Security does not allow the retired workers with Social security as the only source of their income to pay income tax. In 2018, $1,411 was the monthly average Social Security benefits to the retirees. The amount was not above the taxable threshold for an individual.

The Social Security Administration stated in 2018 that about forty percent of the people, who were receiving Social Security benefits, continued to pay income tax to the federal government. But you can avoid paying taxes on your Social Security benefit by; staying below the taxable thresholds, managing other sources of retirement income, saving in a Roth IRA, factoring in state taxes, setting up Social Security tax withholding, and taking IRA withdrawals before enrolling for Social Security.

For many years, setting up social security tax withholding has proved to be one of the best strategies a person can use to avoid

Social Security taxes. Besides, making your quarterly estimated taxes to the IRS, you can also allow Social Security to withhold your federal taxes from your monthly payments. Unfortunately, you cannot decide the percentage to use for your monthly benefits except the one provided by Social Security.

Where we live also plays a significant role in determining if our Social Security payments should be subjected to taxes. The current statistics show that most states in the United States do not impose taxes on workers' Social Security incomes. Only thirteen states are the ones that tax workers. Examples of such states include Missouri, Utah, New Mexico, Montana, and Kansas, among others. Even though these states tax people, they do not impose Social Security tax to the retired workers who are earning a low income.

Windfall Elimination

The majority of people in the United States do not know about "Windfall Elimination." Known as WEP, Windfall Elimination Provision refers to a formula both workers and employers can use to reduce the size of their Social Security retirement benefits, especially if they are receiving a pension. Such a pension should be from the jobs they did not pay taxes (Social Security taxes). This type of pension is normally common if a person has worked for either local government agency or a state that does not involve in FICA tax withholding.

A person collecting such a pension is likely to receive up to half of his Social Security benefit. But the current law does not allow you to be denied your Social security benefit entirely. The Social Security Administration shows that about one-point million people are the victims of this provision.

Historically, the Windfall Elimination Provision (WEP) was approved in 1983 by congress as a part of reforming the Social Security system. Other reforms enacted during that time include normal retirement age and the penalty for delaying your Social Security retirement benefits. The main objective for WEP was to prevent American workers from receiving a non-covered pension, particularly from the local or state employment.

How Does Windfall Elimination Provision Affect Your Benefits

Every provision an individual, institution, or government enacts affects people both positively and negatively. Typically, this provision affects people who are receiving either retirement or disability pension from an organization that does not withhold Social Security taxes. Its application on you will reduce your benefits with a certain amount. It is applied if you have turned age 62, and you became disabled after 1985.

There are some situations in which this provision is not applied to your Social Security benefits. Such exceptions apply if you; are a federal employee who was employed after December 31, 1983, working for a nongovernmental organization, have thirty or more years of substantial earnings, or your first work did not Social Security taxes.

Chapter Seven: Social Security: Family, Spouse, Survivor, and Children

Introduction

Whether in cash or in any other form, child and family benefits have proved to play a vital role in addressing the rights and the needs of children and survivors, especially the disadvantaged families. Several studies not only from the United States but also from other parts of the world show that about twenty million people have benefited from Social Security. In other words, the system has improved the lives of many families and their nutritional status.

Without a doubt, the social security program has also increased the utilization of postnatal health visits, as well as the reduction of home-based births. Reduction in the number of women giving birth from home since this program was launched in the country is a big sign that Social Security benefit is enhancing both maternal and the health of our children.

Whether conditional or non-conditional, Social Security benefits have generally led to the production and provision of better health services. The statistics from the federal government illustrate that unlike it was before the establishment of this system in the country in 1935, our schools, both high schools and colleges, as well as universities, are now experiencing a large number of enrollments. Parents who have enrolled in Social Security and signed an education program for their children are able to take their children to school without strain. Social Security uses channels like children's educational program, child benefits, and family benefits, to improve not only the lives of our children, but also their ability to grab social, economic, and political opportunities. It also uses these forms as a way of responding to children and people with disabilities.

Social Security Benefits for Your Children

Many people across the world assume that Social Security is a program for senior citizens and retirees. They do not know that the system also has another important program that provides help to the disadvantaged members of society. Social Security Administration states that in 2018, about 4 million children received $2.6 billion.

Our children may automatically qualify for Social Security benefits if we die, become disabled, or retire. The benefits are meant to help them pay their school fees. Congress also enacted a law that allows both the dependent children and unmarried one to become eligible for Social Security benefits. However, they must have been under the care of the deceased or disabled grandparents.

Children Qualifying for Social Security Benefits

Not every child qualifies for social security benefits. There are many factors that are put into consideration to determine if he/she is eligible for the program. Either biological and adopted children or even the stepchildren, your children will be eligible to receive the benefits if they meet the following factor;

i. You are either disabled or retired, and you are receiving Social Security benefits
ii. They are not married
iii. They have 19 years and below and are full-time high school students
iv. They became disabled before turning age 22.

How your Children can Receive Social Security Benefits

For your children to receive benefits from Social Security, they must apply in person. The first step to do is to present their birth certificates, their Social Security numbers, and your Social Security number too. Social Security may also require you to provide them with some additional documents about the status of your children. Your children must provide your death certificate or evidence of disability from the medical professionals in order to be accepted.

Do not worry if you have a child with disabilities; Social Security will provide you with both a fact sheet to help you perform the process of getting the benefits with ease. In fact, the information provided in the fact sheet will not only help you sign up for Social Security but also obtain the benefits without any difficulty.

It is important to know that your child, who gets Social Security benefits, is likely to stop receiving the benefit due to reasons, which we will discuss later in this chapter. Remember that you will not continue receiving benefits for your child once he/she turns 16 years. This applies when your kid is not suffering from any disabilities.

The Amount, Your Child, Can Receive as Social Security Benefits

Before enrolling your child for Social Security benefit, it is important for you to know the expected amount your child is likely to receive from the program. Your child can receive even up to half of the amount of your normal retirement benefit. For the deceased parent, the children can get up to seventy-five percent (75%) of their parents' basic Social Security benefit. There is a limit to the total amount that a family is eligible to receive from Social Security.

Moreover, Social Security can pay 150% to 180% family maximum payment of your full benefit amount to all members of the family. But the proportion of every member is reduced in the amount needed to sustain the family exceeds the maximum. Let us take an example of Mike as an elderly parent with a dependent child. The full retirement amount and his family's maximum are $1,500 and $2,300, respectively. From this, it is obvious that Mike would get his $1,500 per month while his wife and the dependent child would share the remaining amount ($800). Each of the family that is his wife and child would get $400 every month. Social Security benefits, in general, are important government tools being used to help children with disabilities or disadvantaged children.

Family Social Security Benefits

Before we discuss Family Social Security benefits, it is important for you to understand what we mean by the term family. Unlike what we understand about the usual definition of the term "family, Social Security uses the term family to refer to individuals who receive benefits. Such benefits should depend on the primary insurance amount of insured workers. For example, both a husband and a wife are counted by Social Security as two distinct families if each is ensured and receives Social Security benefits. But they will be counted as one family if only one of them is insured and receives the benefits. For example, the benefits of a wife, if not ensured, will depend on the number of benefits the husband receives per month, which is always half of what the husband gets.

According to the Social Security Administration, Family Social Security benefits refer to the total amount of benefits your family can collect from Social Security. The amount is always in the form of disability, survivor, retirement, children, and spousal benefits and depends on the earnings history of a single member of the family. Most people call that person a breadwinner.

Do you know how Social Security determines maximum family benefit in case of a breadwinner deceased or is drawing his/her retirement benefit? It is very easy. Social Security will use a formula that yields a figure that is from 150% to 188% of the primary insurance amount of the breadwinner to determine the family's maximum. In fact, your children and spouse may receive auxiliary benefits.

Let us say that you have a spouse and two children who are benefiting from your Social Security record. The family total, together with your payment, is $1,200 more than the maximum. Each of the three will get $400. Note that your benefits will no longer be part of the question if you die.

Married Couples and Social Security Benefits

You have learned that married couples can receive Social Security benefits as a single-family or two identical families depending on various factors, one of them earning their earning records. The time of claiming their benefits also matters a lot. Although married couples are entitled to Social Security benefits if one of them is receiving benefits from Social Security, the amount given to each member cannot more than the monthly benefit of a breadwinner. In order for you to get maximum benefit, you need to prove that you have thirty-five years of working with maximum taxable earnings during that period. However, the maximum payment for an individual who has reached full retirement age as in 2019 is $2,861, according to Social Security Administration. As such, there is a possibility that a married couple can get the maximum retirement benefit, but this depends on their work histories.

Moreover, Social Security does not allow your spouse to collect Social Security benefits on your record if you have not retired or passed on. He/she is only allowed to collect your benefits if you have been receiving Social Security disability or retirement benefit.

The practice of 'file and suspend' ended in 2015 when Congress enacted a new law. Most American married people, according to Social Security Administration, had developed a habit of collecting spousal benefits on their partner's work records, especially those partners who claimed and suspended their Social Security payments by themselves.

Effects of your Spouse's Income on your Social Security retirement benefit

It is important for you to know that the income of your spouse will not affect your Social Security retirement benefit. Social Security allows each spouse to claim their benefits solely based on their earnings history. In fact, both of you can collect your benefits at the same time. Social Security Administration illustrates that your overall amount can be affected by your spouse's earning in some cases, especially if you are receiving payments on the basis of your spouse's earning history.

According to the Social Security Administration, your spouse can only get up to fifty percent (50%) of your primary insurance amount as a benefit. The one claiming spousal benefits, however, must have turned age 66, which is the current full retirement age, for him to get 50% of your Social Security benefits.

The deemed filing rule requires married people to file for their retirement and spousal benefits simultaneously. Any person claiming either retirement benefits or spousal benefits is deemed by Social Security to be claiming both the benefits. You can receive the number of your spousal benefits if your spousal benefits exceed your retirement benefits.

Let us say that both Mike and his spouse are claiming Social Security at their full retirement age. His retirement earnings records show that he has a monthly retirement benefit of $1,200, and his spouse has a $2,000 monthly benefit. It is obvious that the spouse will get half of Mike's benefit, which is $1,000, according to the Social Security Administration. In effect, however, Social Security will ignore this and pays him $1,200 as a retirement benefit.

Now, what happens if a person has a retirement benefit of only $900 per month? In this case, Social Security will pay the person $1,000, which is equivalent to his/her spousal benefit. Although it could be technically considered that Social Security will use $100 of her spouse's record to top on your $900, financial advisors believe that the person will just be getting her spousal benefit.

Possibility of Filing your Social Security at Age 62 and then Turn it to Spousal Benefits

The only situation where you are allowed to file your Social Security at the age of sixty-two and then switch it spousal benefits, according to Social Security, is when your spouse is not receiving the retirement benefits. In this situation, your income and spousal benefits will not be paid by Social Security.

Divorced Spouse

According to current Social Security, your divorced spouse has the right to receive benefits in accordance with your earnings history, regardless if you are remarried. However, your ex must be unmarried, aged 62 or older, and your marriage had lasted for ten years or more. You should know that your divorced spouse is eligible to receive less benefit. First, Social Security pays your ex their retirement benefit if they are eligible for receiving the benefits on their earnings record. They will also get an additional amount if the benefit on your earnings history is higher than theirs.

Family Maximum

Typically, family maximum refers to the number of benefits Social Security payments to the recipient based on the work history of the breadwinner. The amount does not include any other payments. Let us say that you have three children and all of them qualify for social security benefits; you are not supposed to determine the number of benefits that will be coming in by simply adding up their potential benefits since Social Security Administration has put a limit on the number of benefits that should go to each family.

How Family Maximum Works

Now that you have learned about family maximum and it impacts your spouse, it is important for you to know how it works. Normally, the Social Security Administration will reduce the number of secondary benefits if it found out that the total amount of benefits to be paid under a single worker's earnings history is more than the family maximum. In simple terms, it means that your benefits will not be affected or reduced. The only amount to be reduced will be that of your spouse and children or any other eligible members of the family.

If you die and leave behind a spouse who has reached the normal retirement age and three children depending on her, for example, the widow will qualify for one hundred percent of her normal retirement benefit while the three children qualify for seventy-five percent. Adding all will lead to 350 percent of your full retirement benefits. However, the family maximum will significantly reduce the benefits to make it not more than 188% of your full benefits.

Looking at this case from a mechanical view, it is clear that Social Security reduces these benefits using a pro data principle. For example, a surviving spouse and a child are eligible to get $2,000 and $1,500 every month, respectively. The family maximum will be $3,500. Applying family maximum means that both the spouse and the child will receive $1,400 and $1,050 per month. The reduction is, therefore, a reflection of a thirty percent overall cut, which is caused by the family's maximum.

The Impacts of Family Maximum

There are some situations in which you will not see family maximum coming up in your retirement context. This is because of few opportunities for retirees' children who are eligible for social security benefits. The other situation is where there is only a worker and spouse who are eligible for Social Security benefits, and the total amount of benefits is not larger than the family maximum.

The family maximum applies commonly in the context of the survivor. For example, a surviving spouse in a family with many children can receive a benefit of up to 100 percent of the deceased benefit, while eligible children can receive up to seventy-five percent of the benefit. In other words, the family maximum will kick in if the deceased worker has more than one eligible kid.

Survivor Family

Many people do not talk about death because of the impacts it causes to the family. In my view, I believe it is good to think about it, especially if you have already enrolled in Social Security since it offers survivor benefits to help the family that is affected by the death of a person who was earning. You need to consider all the available benefits being offered by Social Security to people who are survivors.

Remember that some of the taxes we pay when we are working and paying to Social Security are used for survivor's insurance. Both your spouse and children or even your parents may be eligible for these benefits depending on the number of your earnings. The program protects you when your parent, adult child, or spouse dies.

Chapter Eight: Social Security: Claims Filing

Introduction

We have seen that Social Security plays many important functions in our lives. It is used to provide a safety net to people who are suffering from an illness, injury, or any other disabilities that can prevent them from working. For example, Social Security achieves these through Social Security disability insurance (SSDI) and Supplemental Security Income (SSI). While SSDI refers to the benefits given to workers who develop a serious long-term disability, the SSI is important to people who have not contributed anything to Social Security due to their inability to work.

Most people in the United States miss out on millions in Social Security benefits every year. This is because most of them make one or several mistakes when they are filling the Social Security claim form. Such mistakes could include not understanding the claim and claiming the benefits that they do not qualify.

In this chapter, we are going to look at aspects, such as claim filing, six Social Security claiming errors you should avoid every time, and how to claim Social Security disability.

Social Security Claiming Errors

In most cases, people find themselves making a lot of mistakes when making Social Security claim. The most common mistake is claiming too early. Although you have learned in the previous chapters that you can claim your retirement benefits before reaching normal retirement age, which is currently sixty-six, according to Social Security Administration. However, the age changes every year, and this could be the main reason why most people get confused when making claims. Social Security allows you to make a claim at the age of 62.

It is important to know that your full benefit will reduce every time you claim benefits if you are not at your normal full retirement age. If you were to receive about $1,000 at your full retirement age and you decide to make a claim fifty months early, your permanent $1,000 will reduce to about $741, which is around twenty-six percent in reduction.

Another reason why most people make mistakes when claiming their benefits is the lack of adequate knowledge about their earning limit. Even though Social Security allows you to receive your Social Security retirement benefits and at the same time, works as either full-time or part-time, it is important for you to know your yearly earning limits before you start filing the claim. Social Security can reduce your benefits if it finds out that you are earning more than your yearly limit.

The current earning limit, according to the Social Security Administration, is $17,000. These values changes every year. Your total benefits will be reduced by one dollar for every two dollars you earn above this limit amount. In fact, the earning limit for a full age claimant can increase up to $46,920. In such cases, the Social Security Administration will deduct one dollar for every three dollars above the limit.

Many people, especially those who work on a full-time basis while collecting their benefits, find themselves in a problem when Social Security informs them that they have made a lot of money and must start repaying some benefits. Therefore, the best thing to do is to start collecting your benefits once you turn your full retirement age.

Thinking that you can turn off your social security and then start your benefit is the biggest mistake most people in the United States do. According to Social Security laws, a person cannot stop his/her social security benefit as easy as possible. He can repay all his benefits within the first twelve months of filing if he decides to change the mind. Generally, try to contact your financial experts before you decide to stop your benefits because you will not be allowed to start again in the future. They will provide you with comprehensive information and advise you on what to do to avoid regretting later in your life.

Moreover, most people are unaware of spousal benefits. Social Security allows spouses to coordinate the claiming of their Social Security benefits. Even though you may think this is not a good idea to you, especially if you do not get financial experts to tell you, you can receive a large number of benefits.

Lastly, some people do not understand the importance of paying taxes on their benefits without knowing that their Social Security benefits will be taxed. The percentage currently use by

Social Security varies from zero to eighty-five percent. So, you can reduce the amount to be taxed on your Social Security retirement benefits if you take enough time the best accounts and time to draw your retirement income.

How to Claim Social Security Disability

The current Social Security report shows that about $143 billion are paid to hundreds of thousands of American people every year. The amount goes only to people who are not working since they are suffering from serious injury, illness, or impairment. The report also reveals that about two-point-seven million applications were received by the Social Security Administration in 2018. The SSA states that the number of people claiming Social Security benefits continues to grow from every year. Although Social Security receives many applications every year, the number of those approved has remained to be slim. For example, the 2018 annual report shows that only thirty-six percent of the applicants were approved in 2018. The remaining did not meet the requirements, even though they were enrolled for Social Security. Congress continues to look for a possible solution that would make the process easy, thus ensuring every applicant gets approved. This is because the process has been experiencing fraudulent claims from many people.

With the current SSDI process, however, applicants are required to get the right materials by themselves at the right time in order to be approved for Social Security disability benefits. As such, the application process has become a job in itself. Applicants are sometimes declined because of early applications or using wrong application materials. In other words, they do not meet the requirements set by the SSDI.

Social Security Disability Insurance (SSDI)

It is good to know that Social Security Disability Insurance is one of the many programs being offered by Social Security to people who cannot work anymore because of the disability. The program gets funds from the FICA tax. It does not only replace the income you lost due to the disability but also helps in keeping your earnings update to enable you to get a large amount of Social Security retirement benefits at your full retirement age.

However, you must work and pay FICA taxes for you to qualify for SSDI. Social Security has a specific law that stipulates the time you will need to pay the FICA taxes. The normal period, according to Social Security Administration, is between five to ten years before the start of your disability. Younger workers have reduced requirements. Self-employed people are also eligible or SSDI only if they pay enough FICA tax.

Regardless of your financial status, it is better to know that you are eligible for Social if you have been paying for the FICA tax. But your SSDI benefits will be reduced by Social Security only if it finds out that you are getting benefits from state disability from the job, which you have never paid Social Security taxes.

Calculation of Your SSDI

Social Security calculates your SSDI benefits based on your earnings history. Therefore, the benefits differ from one person to another; it is not the same since every person has a different earnings record. You will stop receiving your SSDI once you turn age sixty-two years. It is at that time where both Social Security retirement benefits and Medicare benefits are said to take over, according to Social Security Administration.

Unlike other Social Security programs, you will not start receiving your SDDI benefits immediately; you get approved. Your benefits will start after six months are over from the time you became disabled. You will also qualify for Medicare benefits after twenty-four months of receiving your first monthly check if you are receiving SSDI benefits. Do not rush to apply for SSDI; look for a financial expert to help you apply it correctly. This is one of the best reasons you can increase your chances of getting approved into the SSDI program.

Social Security Insurance

Unlike SSDI, Social Security Insurance (SSI) is a program that concentrates on your financial need than your employment record. You need to meet certain financial requirements for you to qualify for this program. It takes into consideration your unearned and earned income, the income of other peoples who are related, or support you when determining your eligibility. In other words, it is a strict program, and you must provide substantial reasons and proves to show that you are in need of financial support before Social Security approves you for this program. The amount an individual receives every month after approval depends on his level of income. He can receive a reduced or maximum monthly benefit.

Qualification for Social Security Insurance

For you to qualify for Social Security Insurance, you need to have sixty-five years and be in need of finance. You can also qualify for the program if you are blind or disabled. Both citizens and residential citizen requirements are considered by Social Security to approve or reject applications.

In general, Social Security Insurance provides people with monthly benefits, which may be increased or reduced depending on the financial situation of the applicant. For example, a report from Social Security shows that $500 was the monthly benefit for individuals in 1999, while the couples were receiving $750 benefits every month. Note that you will receive benefits after being approved for SSI.

Application Process for Social Security Insurance

If it is your first time to apply for Social Security Insurance, then you should not worry. The application process is not as hard as you may be thinking. With your mobile phone, it is possible for you not only to apply for the program but also get information from Social Security. Most people are encouraged to use this process due to its convenience.

From my experience, I would advise you to provide everything in written form, and you should remain with other copies for references for future references. Also, applying in-person provides you with an opportunity to get free advice from the management. You will also get a chance to determine if your documents have errors and are free from omissions.

Moreover, Social Security can sometimes make a special appointment with applicants whose applications are not clear or do not enable them to go through a normal appointment process. Although the Social Security Administration continues to encourage people to apply over the mobile phone, it is important to make an appointment with them if you are not sure or confident about the process. Do not hesitate to contact the senator or any state representatives when SSA declines your in-person appointment because many people have been told that they do not qualify for the program and yet they meet all the SSI requirements.

According to the Social Security Administration, the clerk must take notes every time you appear in-person. Some of the requirements the clerk notes are whether you are disabled or not. Unfortunately, people with invisible disabilities cannot benefit from this program when they physically to the office. You must make your application for Social Security Insurance benefits immediately since the benefits are released from the first day of the application. As an applicant, you can decide to get a protective filing date from your local district.

You should know that there are three forms you must complete before heading for your appointment. These forms are available at any Social Security District offices and include Function Reports, Work History, and Disability Report. We will discuss these forms in our next chapter. However, those people who are unable to complete these forms by themselves can visit any local offices with necessary information. Do not rush to fill these forms if you are not sure as the information you file there determine if you are eligible for Social Security benefits. Furthermore, you must keep all copies of forms, documents, and medical records safe. Also, it is good for you to deliver your application in-person and then obtain a receipt to show that your application has been received. Some applications, especially those made over the telephones, are sometimes not captured in the system, and that is the main reason I advise you to deliver your application in-person.

Chapter Nine: Disability Report, Function Reports, and Work History

Introduction

There is no secret that the application process for Social Security benefits is sometimes longer due to the availability of thousands of open claims in the country. Most people do not know what they need to have in order to apply for Social Security benefits successfully. It is important for you to understand that your involvement in Social Security, particularly with your Social Security Disability Insurance claim will not end after submitting your application to the Social Security office.

In our previous chapters, we have discussed Social security benefits and various programs it offers to the people. It is your responsibility to understand why Social Security may give you some questionnaires to fill before submitting your application. The questionnaires are very important to Social Security as they show your current financial states and age, thus determining your eligibility for Social Security benefits.

After filing your claim, the Social Security Administration assigns your claim to a disability examiner to determine if you have met the requirements. Disability examiner refers to a Social Security officer who will request your medical records before working on your claim. He/she will also request you to provide additional documents if needed to make a sound decision about your application. In this chapter, we discuss Disability Report, Function Reports, and Work History and how these reports are essential to you for the approval of your Social Security disability benefits.

The Disability Report

The current statistic shows that about fifteen percent of the population in the world is living with some forms of disabilities, of which two-to-four percent experience difficulty functioning, according to the World Health Organization (WHO). Similarly, the Social Security Administration states that many people in the United States apply for Social Security disability benefits every year.

First, the Disability Report is very important to you because it shows your disability status. With this Disability Report, for example, it is easy for Social Security Administration to know the place and the date you began receiving your medical treatment. They are also able to know the type of medical treatments you are receiving since you got injured or disabled. In other words, your Disability Report provides not only clear and accurate information but also information that is complete to increase the chances of your claim to be approved.

Social Security requests all people filling the claims to list down their physical and mental disabilities or any impairment. Therefore, it is important for you to make sure that everything you list is accurate and in detail. You can also provide non-obvious impairments like pain, dizziness, and bladder problems. Another thing you should not forget to do when providing your information about your treatments and doctors is listing the names, mobile numbers, and addresses of all the doctors who have been attending to you from the time you got injured or disabled. Most people fail to provide such information, thus making it hard for the Disability examiner to authenticate their information. The best way to make your claim decision much easier and quicker is by providing copies of medical records to Social Security as early as possible. The documents must be from your doctors, hospitals, or any other medical providers. Although most of us expect this process to take a shorter time, a disability analyst is required to confirm if your documents are genuine, thus delaying the approval of your claim. The analysis cannot make any decision before receiving and approving your medical reports. Most medical providers are always slow in providing such information, making more people in the country to suffer a lot. Therefore, it is important for you to provide the documents by yourself to avoid the holding of your claim. Remember that Social Security Administration does not investigate information that that is not stated in your file. So, provide accurate and detailed information.

Working History Report

Your Work History Report is very important for the approval of your claim. It provides information about your past fifteen years of working. When providing information about your work history, it is good to describe in detail your working experience. The information can include any physical or mental tasks that were required to perform every job, especially if you were unable to do those tasks.

There are some jobs that require people to spend a lot of their time standing, and supermarket attendant is a good example of such jobs. If you were doing such jobs and you are now unable to stand for long hours after getting disabled or serious injuries, then it is good for you to list it in detail. This information will make it easy for the Social Security Administration to approve your claim as fast as possible.

According to Social Security Administration, your age plays a significant role in determining if you can still perform your work well. They may approve you for Social Security disability benefits even if you are still fifty years old. The only thing they need to do is to prove that you do not have the necessary skills or education to perform the work.

The Function Report

The majority of people do not know the importance of the Function Report. They get surprised when the Social Security Administration (SSA) requests them to attach this report when submitting their claim. To be precise, Function Report is another essential document that shows your disability effects on your daily work (life).

To make it easy for SSA to process your documents, it is important for you to provide detailed information about your basic daily living activities or any other employment activities that you are not performing at the moment. Also, avoid providing information that will not help to prove that you are disabled. Social Security allows you to provide information about your inability to drive, shop, or to take care of your yard. Other things a person can include in this report, according to Social Security Administration, are the time he/she takes to sit and walk, the ability to lift or carry things, and the ability to perform housework, among others. Do not forget to show how disability or injury changed your daily routine by indicating what you cannot perform nowadays after becoming disabled. However, to prove your claim, Social Security requires you to attach a copy of your recent medical reports to show your disability status. The report must explain how the impairment has affected your work capacity in general. You can request your medical care provider to submit written information to make it easy for Social Security to approve your claim. Many claims are rejected or take time to be processed because the applicants do not provide all the information or documents required.

Disability Determination Services (DDS)

Social Security has a specific department called Disability Determination Services that is responsible for reviewing the claim files and determines whether the applications are approved or declined. The process takes much time due to the large volume of cases and medical documents involved. So, you will need to wait for some months in order to get feedback from the DDS.

How DDS does works? The DDS assigns your case to a disability analyst to review your medical documents. The process involves contacting all the medical sources that you have listed on your Disability Report. Since the process requires a disability analyst to verify all your attached medical documents, he/she may take some months to provide a response to you.

It is important for you to know that an analyst cannot control medical care suppliers. So, this is also another factor that contributes to a long time of reviewing. After receiving the requested information from the relevant medical officers, he/she may decide to invite you to be examined by the relevant physician. The physician is always paid by the Social Security Administration. Your claim will be declined if you miss appearing to the appointment.

What to Do When Your Claim Is Denied

Social Security Administration may accept or decline your claim. The question you should ask yourself is what to do in case your claim is declined by the SSA. If you believe that SSA was wrong to decline your claim, you can still appeal their decision. In the United States, hundreds of thousand people appeal to the decision, and about half of the appealed cases are approved later.

It is important for you to appeal immediately you get a notice of denial. For you to appeal, you need to obtain a certain Form from any Social Security offices or online, fill and then submit it to the relevant office. You can send a simple appeal letter to the Social Security Administration. They will give you the appropriate form to fill in your details and the reasons why you disagree with the decision.

Appealing Process

The four steps in the appeals process include; reconsideration, administrative hearing at the Office of Hearings and Appeals, reviewing by the Appeals Council, and Federal Court.

i. *Reconsideration Step*

Reconsideration is the first step you should take when Social Security declines your claim. In this step, you will be required to file a request for reconsideration form. Do not confuse this with reapplication because reapplying means that you are beginning from scratch. Those who make reapplication loss their original dates of application. Social Security Administration allows a person to request reconsideration within sixty days after receiving a denial notice.

Social Security Administration also expects you to provide a complete report of the Reconsideration Disability. Make sure to provide any additional medical materials, but you do not need to fill these before the filing deadline. With this form, you have an opportunity to provide any new information about your hospitalization, change in your medical conditions, and your doctor's details. The doctor's details include name, phone number, address, and any other important information that can help to approve your claim. You will stand a higher chance to reverse the decision if you provide detailed information. The file is then sent to the DDS office and assigned to a different analyst for reconsideration.

The current statistic from Social Security reveals that the majority of claims are denied at this stage. SSA requires those who are appealing to provide strong and substantial evidence that were not present in their original claim in order to reverse the decision. However, do not worry about what you receive from SSA again. You must remain focused and determined, even if the Social Security Administration does not reverse the decision. Just proceed to Administration Hearing.

ii. *Administrative Hearing*

Many claims, which are not approved by Social Security Administration at the reconsideration stage, are approved at this stage. It is important for you to meet in-person with the people who decide if your claim should be approved or denied. This not only makes it easy for you to present facts that could not be in your medical records but provides witness to testify about your disability that is preventing you from working.

As a financial expert, who has handled several cases on the claim, I would advise you to look for help from an attorney with extensive knowledge in Social Security Administration and disability claims to represent you during the hearing. It is better to take the attorney to work on your case even if he/she takes a certain percentage, which you must pay if you win the case. The normal fee is twenty-five percent of the retroactive benefit. Social Security allows you to represent yourself, but this is not good, according to my experience. Most people who represent themselves at the hearing end up losing their claims.

Social Security Administration requires a person to file a "Request for Hearing" within sixty days of the reconsideration denial. The filed form sent to the Hearing and Appealing office is then assigned to an Administrative Law Judge to handle the case. You will get a notification twenty days before you attend your hearing. There are many appeals at this point; thus, you should not expect your hearing date to be within a month.

The decision is normally made at this point within ninety days after receiving all the evidence or information, though it may take a longer time depending on the situation and workloads. It is not obvious that you will receive a favorable decision even if you have hired a specialized attorney. In case you get an unfavorable decision, you are allowed to appeal your claim to the Appeals Council.

Appeals Council

Once OHA declined your claim, you have sixty days to file a review. You need to request and fill the form, called *"Request for Review of Hearing Decision,"* and submit it be reviewed by the Appeals Council. At this point, the Appeals Council may decide to uphold, modify the decision made by ALJ, or reverse the decision **Chapter Ten: Social Security Amendments**

Introduction

Since its establishment, Social Security has been serving two main purposes; helping low-income people and those who are suffering from both physical and mental problems. As such, the number of people who have been enrolling for the program has increased nowadays. In fact, Social Security Administration estimates that the number could double by the end of 2032. With the current large number of people applying for retirement benefits, many people are now wondering if Social Security will be able to meet these demands in the future. It is estimated that the number of American people with over sixty-five years will reach twenty percent by 2030. In fact, that is the year when the United States is expected to have a higher number of old people. The full retirement age, for example, was 62 in 2008, allowing many people in the country to be eligible to receive early Social Security retirement benefits. Social Security began experiencing a cash deficit from 2010. Social Security Administration is now focusing on how to reform the system to ensure it meets its goal in the face of economic, demographic, and social trends. To meet its current obligations and cover the deficit, Social Security began to use money from its reserve, and the government estimates that trust funds will be able to cover this deficit for ten years.

Generally, the Social Security Act was enacted in 1935 to establish a national plan that would not only offer economic security to American workers but also enable the states to provide welfare benefits to all eligible people fairly. This chapter discusses why Social Security was seen as a reform, amendments that have been made on the system from the time it was established, and why the Social Security system is still very important in the United States.

Why the Social Security Act was Seen as a Reform

Established in 1935 during the reign of Franklin D. Roosevelt, a U.S President, Social security has improved the lives of many people in the world. It benefits workers with disabilities or impairments and their families. Children with blind and other physical impairments also benefit from this program.

Before the establishment of the Social Security system in the 1930s, it was the responsibility of the locals and families to provide financial support to the elderly. Only veterans received support, which was in the form of a pension from the federal. The Great Depression, however, caused a lot of suffering not only in the United States but also in the entire world. As such, Congress came up with numerous proposals to establish an insurance system. The bill was passed in the two houses and signed by President Roosevelt in 1935 to make the lives of low-income earners better.

The establishment of this act created a unique solution to the problem, which most Americans were going through. It was unique in that Americans contributed to it in the form of taxes. In fact, Americans could not feel its pain since the money was taxed from their earnings. The act authorized Social Security Administration, at that time, called the Social Security board to start enrolling citizens for Social Security benefits. Other functions of the Social Security Administration were to release payment to the beneficiaries and to administer all contributions sent to the Federal Government.

1939 Social Security Amendments

Without a doubt, the 1939 amendments impacted the operation of the Social Security system at large. Social Security began to protect the family rather than protecting individual workers. In fact, it placed more emphasis on different ways of providing benefits to Americans socially. It also affected the financing program. For example, children under age 16 became eligible for this program.

After the enactment of this amendment, Social Security started calculating benefits based on a person's average monthly benefit instead of cumulative lifetime earnings. According to the provision, the shift was because Social Security was only to replace wages lost. At that time, the majority of Americans enrolled in the program. Social Security reports show that about ten million people were registered for Social Security benefits in 1936.

1950 Social Security Amendments

These amendments not only expanded the operation of Social Security but also the scope of Survivors Insurance. About ten million additional American workers were covered in this program after the 1950 amendments. Furthermore, the amendments also increased the amount of benefit and the maximum amount of earnings. The full retirement age changed from 62 to 65.

The amendments covered domestic workers and self-employed workers, as well as federal employees who were working on temporary mode. With these amendments, both locals and states came up with strategies to register citizens. In fact, the conditions for registering a person into Social Security were liberalized since an individual was only required to have quarters of coverage. Just like the workers who were covered under the original Social Security Act, newly covered workers were also eligible for Social Security benefits. The provisions also offered $160 per month as free wage credits for military service. Lastly, the amendments led to the creation of a new formula for computing the average monthly earnings of each worker to ensure that even new workers receive benefits according to their earning records.

1952 Social Security Amendments

Social Security experienced some changes in 1952. The amendments included increasing Social Security benefits by twelve-point five percent and raised the earnings test limit to $75 per month. The changes were not only meant to curb the high number of Americans who were enrolling in the program but also to reduce the poverty level in the country.

The 1954 Social Security Amendments

In 1954, Congress made several amendments that allowed Social Security to cover home-workers and self-employed. Also, the amendments extended coverage to both the local government and state workers. The only state workers who were not covered even after the enactment of these provisions were police officers and firemen. The amendments also gave the ministers an opportunity to enroll for Social Security benefits as self-employed people.

The amendments made it easy for the Social Security Administration to start protecting workers against their incomes, which used to get lost after getting disabled. Before the enactment of the 1954 provisions, workers were not eligible for retirement benefits when they became disabled while working. Those who remained insured received low benefits because the computation of their benefits included the period they were not earnings.

It is important to know that disability, according to the Social Security Administration, referred to a lack of ability to involve in any gainful activities. Workers with disabilities included those with physical or mental challenges, which necessarily prevented them from performing their daily tasks as normal.

Social Security Administration experienced some challenges when it came to determining if the disability was temporary or permanent. As such, the 1954 amendments provided clear guidelines on how the Social Security Administration would determine if a person had been suffering from any injuries or illness for at least six months. In fact, the state was given the responsibility to make determinations of disability.

Many American workers were benefiting from Social Security disability benefits. The 1954 Social Security's report shows that about ten million workers applied for disability benefit in 1953. Congress, however, limited the number by imposing additional insured status requirements. For example, an individual was required to have at least six quarters of coverage for him/her to qualify for disability benefits.

Furthermore, the amendments reduced the normal retirement age from seventy-five to seventy-two years. That was the age at which a worker was paid his/her benefits without necessarily looking at the amount of his/her earnings. In fact, it established an annual earning test that was uniform for both self-employed people, as well as low-earners.

Lastly, the amendments provided the Social Security Administration with a new benefit formula. The formula did not consider four years of your lowest earnings; instead, it considered five years of your earnings if you had 20 quarters of coverage.

The 1956 Social Security Amendments
Unlike the previous amendments, the 1956 amendments came with many benefits to the lives of many workers in the United States. It provided monthly benefits to all disabled employees who were aged between fifty to sixty-five years. Unfortunately, the amendments did not consider the dependents or families of the disabled workers.

However, the amendments required workers to be fully insured and twenty quarters of coverage for them to qualify for disability benefits. They had to wait for six months after applying for the benefit for them to start receiving their payments. The Disability benefit was reduced if Social Security realized that a recipient was also receiving another federal benefit. The recipients were required by the new law to accept rehabilitation services that the states offered to them.

The Disability Insurance trust fund was established by the legislation to help in financing the new benefits. For example, both employers and employees had to contribute an additional tax of 0.25 percent, while self-employed people contributed 0.375% more than the previous contributions. Lastly, amendments came up with a new benefit formula that did not put into consideration five years of workers' earnings regardless of the situation.

The 1958 Social Security Amendments

With these provisions, Social Security was able to increase benefits by seven percent, raise earnings base to $4,800, increase scheduled payroll to four-point-five percent, and allowed dependents of the disabled workers to receive benefits. The amendments also permitted Social Security to pay the disability benefits retroactively for twelve months. However, it was allowed to do so if an applicant had met all the other requirements.

The 1960 Social Security Amendments

Social Security underwent through some challenges in their operation. As such, the congress decided to enact certain provisions to make it easy for Social Security to run its operation without any difficulty. The amendments allowed workers with disabilities to qualify for Social Security benefits at any age. In other words, the provisions did not limit the age limit for disabled workers to qualify for the benefits.

1961 Social Security Amendments

The amendments did not only bring many changes to the structure of Social Security but also to its operation. The retirement age limit for males was reduced to sixty-two (62). That was the age at which one was allowed to collect his/her benefits. However, the number of benefits one could collect after reaching the full retirement age was also reduced. In fact, the amendments changed the requirements an individual had to meet for him/her to get fully insured status. Lastly, the amount of money taxed on both employers and employees increases by one-eighth percent. The minimum benefit was also raised to $40.

1965 Social Security Amendments

Established in 1965, the amendments offered basic protection against the high cost of hospital and any other health-related costs. They also led to the establishment of Medicare Part A (Health Insurance) and Part B (Hospital Insurance). Both Part A and Part B caused workers to incur additional tax. However, Social Security did not force any worker to enroll in these programs. Additionally, the amendments changed the earning test to allow the recipient to earn up to $1,500 every year, and at the same time, still receives his/her benefits. However, the earning was to be withheld by $2 of employee's annual earnings if his/her yearly earnings exceed $1,500.

The provisions also liberalized the meaning of the term disability. For example, in individual became eligible for disability benefits if he/she had suffered from any serious injuries, illness, accidents, or any other physical and mental challenges that affected his/her ability to perform daily work. The amendments also reduced the number of disability benefits to all workers if their benefits and compensation exceeded their previous earnings by eighty percent.

With the amendments, the divorced wives or widows became eligible for Social Security benefits. But they were required to prove that they were real dependents of the deceased or retired workers.

The 1966 Social Security Amendments

In 1966, Congress decided to make some adjustments to the Social Security system. The amendments not only helped in providing benefits but also benefited people who were over seventy-two years old. To be eligible for this special payment, workers were required to have turned age 72 before 1968.

The 1967 Social Security Amendments

The amendments had a great impact on both the operation and financial management of the Social Security program. They increased the number of benefits by thirteen percent, thus increasing the amount each person could earn per year to $1,680. Both widows and dependent widows became eligible for monthly cash benefits after turning fifty years. According to the 1967 amendments, disability included people who were not able to carry out their daily activity while the definition of the surviving spouses remained stricter.

Due to these amendments, young workers did not find it hard to enroll for Social Security benefits. They were not required to have twenty quarters of coverage as it used to be before the enactment of these amendments. For example, it allowed workers with thirty years and below to be insured.

1969 Social Security Amendments

The 1969 amendments did not have many impacts on the Social Security system. It only increased the number of benefits each worker was to receive by fifteen percent.

1971 Social Security Amendments

Just like the 1969 amendments, Social Security amendments of 1971 led to an increase in the level of benefits by ten percent. The earnings base also increased to $9,000. Social Security also increased the tax rate from 5.9 to 6.05% for each employer and employee. But the taxes did not affect self-employed people.

1972 Social Security Amendments

Unlike the previous amendments, the 1972 amendments came with the "indexing" concept. The concept was also known as automatic adjustments to the Social Security program. In fact, any change in the benefits was directly tied to the cost of living. Under these amendments, the benefits automatically increased every January when inflation rose by three percent. Consumer Price Index (CPI) was used by the Social Security Administration to measure the inflation rate. Also, the amendments allowed for automatic adjustment of earnings test as it was the only way to keep pace with any changes in wage levels.

Furthermore, people who had worked in the covered employment for several years at a low amount (wages), under these amendments, were provided with special minimum benefits. The benefit was different from the previous one because it was proportional to the period that covered an individual's earning.

Unlike the previous amendments, the 1972 amendments led to the establishment of the Supplemental Security Income program, which replaced former federal grants. The program was created to aid people with disabilities that were getting a low income.

1973 Social Security Amendments

These amendments led to an increase in the OASDI benefits by eleven percent as an ad hoc adjustment, which was developed to reduce the time spend when compensating workers. Also, the earning base increased to $13,000.

1977 Social Security Amendments

Various studies in 1973 began to show that Social Security could face a financial problem because of a large number of people who were enrolling for Social Security benefits. To estimate any current and future financial problems, the Social Security Administration proposed various changes to the system.

Some of the problems Social Security was experiencing during that time came as a result of adverse economic conditions. The world was experiencing a higher inflation rate, which increased the unemployment rate. Social Security Administration also realized that the long-term problems were being caused by some unfavorable demographic trends. To be precise, the main cause of fiscal deficit was the assumption made about the change in economic conditions in the future. For example, the 1972 amendment laws caused future benefit levels to depend highly on the relationship between price growth and wages.

After the enactment of the 1977 amendments by Congress, Social Security was able to lessen these problems since the amendments significantly changed the benefit formula. With these actions, the Social Security Administration was able to estimate the financial condition properly. The 1977 amendments also increased the tax rates. For example, each employee and employer was taxed a rate of seven-point-six-five percent. The earning base also increased to $29,700 by 1981 but adjusted after 1981.

1980 Social Security Amendments

Before proposing these amendments, Social Security was spending a lot of their financial resources on people. The congress, however, decided to enact these laws not only to control the expenditure but also other issues that were emerging from the management of the Disability Insurance program. The amendments led to the establishment of a limit on the disability family benefit. They also provided Medicare coverage. As a worker, you were covered for at least thirty-six months after Social Security had stopped providing you with cash benefits. The coverage was only provided to those workers who were engaging in gainful activities. Workers who were previously receiving medical benefits and became disabled or injured for the second time had to wait for a period of twenty-four months for them to start receiving the benefits again. Lastly, the Social Security secretary had to review the status of all the disabled people every three years to determine if they should continue getting disability benefits.

1981 Social Security Amendments

Social Security experienced budgetary pressures in 1981. They decided to come up with proposals to reduce or eliminate some of the types of benefits. The amendments provided for the removal of minimum benefits for future recipients. Social Security Administration projected that the amendments would enable the system to solvent for fifty years.

Unfortunately, economic performance became worse in the 1980s than what was projected by the SSA, causing a rapid decline in the trust fund reserves. To asses and control the situation, Congress enacted stopgap measures that led to the government reallocating revenues between the DI trust funds and the OASI during that time. Social Security was given authority to borrow money from the government or any other institution.

1983 Social Security Amendments

Social Security was still experiencing some financial problems even after the enactment of the 1981 amendments. Reagan, a president of the United States at that time together with congressional leaders, passed a motion that led to the formation of a bipartisan panel. Even though some members of the bipartisan panel did not agree with the decision, the majority of them agreed on a compromise solution. They agreed that Social Security should reduce the benefits each recipient was receiving. According to them, this was one of the best ways Social Security could use to solve the short-term financing problems.

The recommendations were incorporated by Congress in 1983. Congress also provided some modifications and other additional provisions to solve the long-term deficit. The provisions made it mandatory for all people who were working in a non-governmental organization to be covered. No organization, whether the non-governmental or governmental organization, was allowed to terminate the coverage after 1982.

1984 Social Security Amendments

The economic hardship of 1984 raised many concerns to Congress. Congress enacted laws that required the Social Security Administration to monitor the qualifications or benefit payments made to any person who was not a spouse.

1985 Social Security Legislation

Unlike many previous amendments, 1985 was so unique in that the president had the authority to reduce federal expenditures, particularly those that could lead to the budget deficit. With these amendments, it was difficult for either the House or Senate to make some changes to Social Security during the congressional budget process as it used to be before.

1986 Social Security Amendments

The rate of inflation slowed down in 1986. This, however, made Congress eliminate the three percent requirement permanently. The three percent requirement was the one that authorized one-point-three percent COLA.

1987 Social Security Amendments

The 1987 amendments lengthened the period of allowing disability recipients to be eligible for the benefit. The required period was fifteen to thirty-six months.

1989 Social Security Amendments

Unlike the previous amendments, the 1989 amendments gave children who were adopted after a person the opportunity to receive Social Security benefits.

1990 Social Security Amendments

After the enactment of these amendments, the recipient could choose to continue receiving both Medicare and disability benefits. It also extended benefits to spouses who were living with workers before workers passed on. Also, the trust fund was removed from the calculation of the budget deficit. In fact, Congress enacted new laws that helped in protecting trust fund balances.

Chapter Ten: Financing Social Security

Introduction

For many years, most Social Security systems in the world have been operating on the basis of pay-as-you-earn. Most people think that these programs will become unaffordable and inefficient or even ineffective in the future. Various studies have revealed that both the aging populations and competitive forces in the new global economy can make Social Security experience financial problems later.

Financial experts assert that the financial sustainability of the Social Security system can help us to realize the importance of enrolling for Social Security if it is discussed in the context of increased longevity and mobility. However, there is a need to consider structural changes in the employment structure and casual work, as well as labor force participation.

Although most people think that Social Security cannot operate well at the time of adjustment periods, there are other options, even in developing countries. The methods include increasing tax revenues, re-allocating public expenditure, lobbying for transfer and aid, expanding social security coverage, restructuring the existing debt, eliminating illicit financial flows, and using fiscal and foreign exchange reserves.

The government can use either one of these options or all the options to expand fiscal space, thus generating the necessary resources for Social Security. But it is the responsibility of your government to enact policy or laws to support these financing options.

Social Security Administration continues to witness a large number of people enrolling for Social Security. In order to operate effectively, Social Security gets funds from sources, such as non-governmental organizations, national governments, employees, and employers. With these sources of finance, Social Security has managed to reach thousands of million people regardless of their age and gender, thus demonstrating how the government is committed to investing in her people. In fact, this results in the formation of mutual obligations where all people are living in the country pay taxes to the state to receive benefits and services.

About seventy percent of the countries use taxes to finance their Social Security systems since most of the citizens are in the informal sectors. It is important to know that Social Security rarely covers those people working in the informal sectors and gets low wages on an irregular basis. The wages are always paid in cash, making it hard for taxation. Therefore, the government depends highly on the formal sector, where it is easy to obtain the tax.

How Government Finance Social Security

The government must provide financial support to Social Security to enable them to provide income security for older persons, children, and older people who are still working to reduce the level of poverty in society. With financial support from the government, the Social Security Administration believes that the level of poverty in the United States will reduce to 1% by the end of 2030. The government uses ways such as public expenditure, regulation, macroeconomic policy, and tax policy to support Social Security.

The government can enact various macroeconomic policies that will ensure both fiscal stability and sustainable growth not only to reduce vulnerability but also to secure resources that are necessary for the operation of Social Security. Also, effective social security helps in achieving macroeconomic goals as it contributes to an adaptable economy that utilizes globalization effectively. It is, therefore, important to have a macroeconomic policy that not only prevents macroeconomic crises but also reduces their impacts on the poor. To achieve this, most governments are nowadays building capacity for an autonomous fiscal policy.

Additionally, tax policy is another important element in supporting Social Security financially. The policy not only provides direction on how social security should collect its revenue to finance public expenditure but also support it through tax expenditure. With proper tax policy, it is easy for Social Security Administration to determine the exact amount of money (revenues) it will gain at the end of each year.

Regulations are used to cover areas, such as employee benefits, price regulation, and labor standards.

Moreover, SSA has a mandate to collect payroll taxes. The money collected is used to pay survivors, disability, and retirement benefits. The value of trust funds increases when Social Security runs a surplus. For example, the Trust Fund had about $2.79 trillion in 2014. The government uses excess funds for another purpose, thus creating obligations to both the recipients and the SSA. Congress can, however, reduce these obligations by making some adjustments or altering the laws. Even though the majority of people have developed behavioral responses against payroll tax, there is a need to make them understand the importance of paying taxes into social security. First, your money is always safe when you pay into Social Security since they are returned to you in the form of benefits. In case of death, your spouse or children will be eligible to receive them. It is also important for individuals to know that Social Security is another way of savings.

Payroll Taxes as a Source of Finance to Social Security

The amount is then paid to retirees, disabled workers, and their families in the form of benefits. For example, it is reported that about 63.3 million people currently benefit from Social Security. All the covered workers and employers pay payroll taxes, which is the main source of finance, into Social Security. Under the current law, each employer or employee is supposed to contribute five-point-three percent of the taxable wages, of which zero-point nine percent goes to FICA taxes. Even though up to $12,400, according to Social Security Administration, is subjected to FICA taxes, and the amount varies every year, Medicare tax does not have any wage cap. In fact, these taxes have enabled Social Security to operate effectively.

Other Sources of Finance

In addition to payroll taxes, Social Security has been receiving funds from beneficiaries with income more than the threshold. Such revenues are remitted to the DI and OASI or HI trust funds. The best thing with a trust fund is that it earns interest. Congress can sometimes enact laws that enable the addition of money to the trust funds from the general funds directly. Between 2011 and 2012, the general funds were used to reimburse the trust funds after payroll tax was suspended temporarily by the government as a stimulus measure.

• *Re-allocation of Public Expenditure*

It is another source of financing Social Security program and includes careful assessment of on-going budget allocations. It helps in tackling corruption and eliminating unnecessary spending. In 1983, for example, Congress formed a committee to investigate how the economic crisis was affecting the operation of Social Security. Increasing the normal retirement age limit was one of the amendments that were seen to be effective as Congress believed that the majority of Americans were applying for early retirement benefits.

• *Tax Revenues Increase*

Increasing tax revenues is another way of generating resources for Social Security. It is achieved through different types of tax rates on corporate profits, property, imports, and exports, and financial activities. Most countries across the world increase tax not only on consumption but also in other areas. The money collected is then given to social security in order to operate effectively. For example, Maldives introduced taxes on tourism when the Social Security program was running out of money. The money was used to support the program.

• *Expanding Both Contributory Revenues and Social Security Coverage*

Most governments across the world have realized that increasing coverage can be the most effective and reliable approach to financing Social Security. This approach ensures that there is a free fiscal space for other social expenditures. For example, the United States and other countries, including Argentina and Brazil, have broadened social security coverage and contributions.

Social Security Trust Fund

Although Social Security payroll tax is the main source of revenue of Social Security, both federal income taxes and interest on the fund's investment holdings are the other sources of income to Social Security. It is good to remember that payroll tax contains twelve-point-four percent (12.4%) of the total tax on the wages. The percentage, however, is not always constant; it varies each year.

How to Measure the Operation of Social Security Trust Fund

We can measure the operation of trust fund using methods, such as the accumulated holdings and the annual cash flow operations. Let us explain each method in detail and how it works. The annual cash flow operations are defined as the measures of both the current costs and revenues. They are always positive when the amount of positive revenues is more than the amount of cash flow surplus. But it will be negative if the revenue is less than the current costs. Unlike other federal programs, Social security programs can use the accumulated holdings to pay benefits to the recipients and other administrative expenses if there is a deficit in the cash flow surplus. For example, Social Security had more than $3 trillion of accumulated holdings by the end of 2018, according to Social Security trustee's annual report. In fact, the report estimates that the trust funds will continue to have a positive balance until 2035.

Understanding the noninterest income-yearly cost ratio is an effective way of measuring the level of cash flow operation. Positive cash flow is indicated by the ratio that is greater than one hundred percent, while negative cash flow is shown by a ratio of less than one hundred percent. Previously, you learned that your social security benefit is calculated according to your average earning history. So, it is this amount that is used to determine the cash flow operation.

What Happens When Trust Funds Run Out

Most people, especially self-employed, do not like to enroll for Social Security due to fear that it could run out of cash if there is economic inflation. In fact, they concentrate on the projection year on which Social Security trust funds are estimated to become solvent. Most of us were surprised by the Social Security trustees' 2018 annual report, which stated that the disability insurance and OASI trust funds are expected to be exhausted in 2019 and 2032, respectively, under the current laws. Even though the two funds are always described in combination, they are separated by laws.

A majority of the population believes that Social Security will not be able to pay any benefits if the trust funds get exhausted.

This is not true. Social Security has got many other sources of funds and will never run out of cash, even during the economic crisis. It is believed that Congress would enact laws to effect the reduction in the number of benefits that would be paid to the beneficiaries during that time. Social Security can decide to make reduce the payments or delay payment schedule.

With the annual Social Security report, it is easy for you to know how the program operates and manages its finance effectively. In fact, the report not only explains in detail the current operation of Social Security trust funds but also describes the projected future operations of the Social Security trustees. It also provides information on what could take place if Congress allows the trust funds to exhaust. Generally, policymakers can restore such a problem by raising the rate of payroll tax and reducing the number of benefits paid to each Social Security recipient.

Social Security and Future Funding

According to the Social Security Administration, there is a little reason why the system might expect its funding sources to change in the future. Most financial advisors believe that the current increase in the number of people who are receiving Social Security benefits will lead to an increase in the amount of taxes taxed on the benefits in 2024. Also, the rate of payroll taxes will grow faster than that of total funding. The changes could be because of the economic crisis. But this should not stop you from enrolling for Social Security benefits.

Payroll taxes, without any doubt, will continue to be an important part of Social Security regardless of what the program goes through. The amount taxed on the employers and employees is used to fund the aging population, thus increasing their incomes. It is important to know that the amount we pay for Social Security does not go to our personal accounts but is used to pay those who have attained the minimum retirement ages.

Conclusion

Although there are many other financial programs in the United States, Social Security has remained to be the foundation of economic security for many Americans. Most people benefiting from the program include the retired workers and disabled people, as well as families of the deceased or disabled workers. Nowadays, more than 169 million Americans are paying Social Security taxes, where sixty-one million receive Social Security benefits.

Since its establishment, Social Security has undergone several changes, and this has continued to improve its public image. For example, the 1983 Amendments increased the normal retirement age to sixty-seven from sixty-five. The amendments also imposed penalties on those people who were applying for early retirement benefits. As such, a large number of Americans suffered a lot as their benefits were permanently reduced.

Under the current Social Security laws, you can increase your monthly benefits by increasing your pre-retirement and post-retirement earnings, as well as delaying your retirement age. It is also important to know that workers with ten years of covered earnings and have turned sixty-five years are eligible for Social Security retirement benefits. In fact, such workers are not subjected to payroll if their earnings have exceeded the covered earnings maximum, which varies every year. After initiating the benefits, the Social Security Administration will calculate your primary insurance amount as a function of your covered earning records.

Your spouse and children are also eligible to receive Social Security benefits when you die or retire. The number of benefits they will receive will depend on your earning history too. Just like you, your spouse will be allowed to collect spousal benefits after turning sixty-two. Unfortunately, there is no increase in benefits, even if your spouse decides to delay the benefits.

For an individual to qualify for Social Security Disability Insurance (SSDI), a person is required to have obtained enough work credits. The amount of credits you earn depends on the type of work you are doing. For example, some jobs are covered under this program and enable you to earn four credits at the end of each year. You can also qualify for Social Security disability insurance with six credits, even if you are twenty-four years and below. However, the Social Security Administration requires each applicant to provide medical documents to prove that he/she is unable to perform the work or is disabled. They can schedule an in-person appointment with you to determine if you are really disabled.

Unfortunately, Social Security will not consider you for disability benefits if you are earning more than $1,000 each month from your employment. The good thing is that Social Security does not have a limit on the amount of your unearned income. The amount of benefits Social Security gives a person every month depends on his/her work history and cannot change at any time. Furthermore, Social Security does not prevent individuals from receiving disability benefits from getting other Social Security income (SSI). By definition, SSI refers to the benefit given to a person who has limited means of obtaining income and is blind or has sixty-five years and above. The program allows disabled people who are not qualified for SSDI due to lack of work credits to also receive the benefits since it has limits on both the income and resources. As such, you will not qualify for the SSI program if you have more than $2,000 in your bank account.

However, some Americans prefer applying for Medicare to Social Security benefits, while others take both programs. It is easy for an individual to enroll in this program even if you are not willing to go for retirement. With a computer or a smartphone in your palm of your hand, you can apply for Medicare online, and the process takes at least ten minutes since the system does not request you to submit any documents. After applying for Medicare, Social Security processes all the applications and sends the response in applicants' respective emails. They can request more information from you, but this depends on various factors.

There are two main types of Medicare you can enroll in when applying for Medicare. They include Part A, which is also called Hospital Insurance and Part B, Medical Insurance. An applicant must pay the Medical Insurance premium. However, this should not stop you from applying for Medicare. Some people turn Medical Insurance down during application. Unfortunately, such people may end up paying a late enrollment penalty if they decide to enroll for medical insurance coverage.

As an independent organ under the management of the federal government, Social Security continues to oversee all insurance programs in the country. The insurance programs are in the form of survivor benefits, disability benefits, and retirement benefits, among others. The disability benefit is provided to people who have medical documents showing that they can no longer perform their work.

Even though all people can apply for Social Security, there is a requirement one must meet in order to be approved for Social Security benefit. An individual must have at least sixty-two years and obtained the full forty credits. Young children with twenty-four years and below are eligible for the benefits.

Moreover, Social Security is vital in reducing the level of poverty among seniors. The 2018 American statistic shows that about twelve percent of the American elderly are living a poor life. The number will increase to fifty percent if Social Security stops offering retirement benefits to them.

Lastly, our national governments can support Social Security systems through tax policy, regulations, macroeconomic policy, and public expenditure. For example, macroeconomic not only contribute to sustainable growth but also to fiscal stability. They also help in securing the resources required for Social Security, thus reducing vulnerability.

Thanks for Reading!

What did you think of, *Social Security: The New Rules, Essentials & Maximizing Your Social Security, Retirement, Medicare, Pensions & Benefits Explained In One Place*

I know you could have picked any number of books to read, but you picked this book and for that I am extremely grateful. I hope that it added at value and quality to your everyday life. If so, it would be really nice if you could share this book with your friends and family by posting to Facebook and Twitter.

If you enjoyed this book and found some benefit in reading this, I'd like to hear from you and hope that you could take some time to post a review. Your feedback and support will help this author to greatly improve his writing craft for future projects and make this book even better.

Please keep in touch with me or for questions and advice:
wswainpublishing@gmail.com

Thank you and good luck!
Peter Allen

Download the Audio Book Version of This Book FREE

If you love listening to audio books on-the-go, I have great news for you. You can download the audio book version of this book for FREE just by signing up for a FREE 30-day audible trial! See below for more details!

Audible trial benefits

As an audible customer, you'll receive the below benefits with you 30-day free trial:

- Free audible copy of this book
- After the trial, you will get 1 credit each month to use on any audiobook
- Your credits automatically roll over to the next month if you don't use them
- Choose from Audible's 200,000 titles
- Listen anywhere with the audible app across multiple devices
- Make easy, no hassle exchanges of any audiobook you don't love
- Keep your audiobooks forever, even if you cancel you membership

And much more

References

Burtless, G., & Aaron, H. (2013). *Closing the Deficit: How Much Can Later Retirement Help?* Brookings Institution Press.

Gruber, J., & Wise, D. A. (2008). *Social Security and Retirement around the World*. University of Chicago Press.

Hoefer, R., & Midgley, J. (2013). *Poverty, Income, and Social Protection: International Policy Perspectives*. London, England: Routledge.

III, D. A. (2016). *Nolo's Guide to Social Security Disability: Getting & Keeping Your Benefits*. Berkeley, CA: Nolo.

Matthews, J. (2018). *Social Security, Medicare, and Government Pensions: Get the Most Out of Your Retirement and Medical Benefits*. Berkeley, CA: Nolo.

Moulta-Ali, U. (2010). *Disability Benefits Available Under the Social Security Disability Insurance and Veterans Disability Compensation Programs*. Collingdale, PA: DIANE Publishing.

National Research Council, Division of Behavioral and Social Sciences and Education, Board on Behavioral; Cognitive; and Sensory Sciences, & Committee on Disability Determination for Individuals with Visual Impairments. (2002). *Visual Impairments: Determining Eligibility for Social Security Benefits*. Washington, DC: National Academies Press.

Saunders, P. (2019). *Revisiting Henderson: Poverty, social security, and basic income*. Melbourne Univ. Publishing.

Schieber, S. J. (2012). *The Predictable Surprise: The Unraveling of the U.S. Retirement System*. Oxford University Press.

Wright, H. (2013). *The Complete Guide to Creating a Special Needs Life Plan: A Comprehensive Approach Integrating Life, Resource, Financial, and Legal Planning to Ensure a Brighter Future for a Person with a Disability*. London, England: Jessica Kingsley Publishers.

www.ingramcontent.com/pod-product-compliance
Lightning Source LLC
Chambersburg PA
CBHW030300030426
42336CB00009B/458